APARTMENT 10-D

Verly E. Dolce

Copyright © 2020, Verly E. Dolce. All rights reserved.

Verly E. Dolce asserts the moral right to be identified as the author of this book. Without limiting the rights under copyright reserved above, no part of this book may be reproduced in any form or by any electronic or mechanical means, including information storage and retrieval systems, without prior permission in writing from the publisher, except by a reviewer who may quote brief passages in a review.

Paperback ISBN 978-0-9971257-5-7
Ebook ISBN 978-0-9971257-6-4
Audio ISBN 978-0-9971257-7-1

Library of Congress Control Number: 2020907393

Book and Cover Design by Blue Jay Ink, Ojai, California

Published in the United States by
Blue Jay Ink, 451A East Ojai Avenue, Ojai, CA 90302
bluejayink.com

- Dedication -

This memoir is dedicated to all of Earth's inhabitants who are currently suffering.
I feel your pain, I share your pain.
Rest assured, the day will come when the agony will end and absolution will be yours.
Keep your heads up, you will be free soon enough.
You will be vindicated soon enough. I'm sending positive vibes to you all.

- Acknowledgments -

Grandma Rose, I love you, I miss you. Many thanks to the individuals and families who took me in when my own spurned me. The following families hold a very special place in my heart; Mme Daniel's, Bazile, Darius, Tassy-Orjiugo, Augustine, Francois, Joseph, Philogene-Bretoux-Renaud, Lopez, Nordahl, Cuellar-Puerto, Torres-Camacho, Brenord.. Just to name some of them; forgive me if I didn't mention you, know that you're still in my heart.

I would also like to thank those of you who have wronged me. I learned some of life's most valuable lessons because of you. I thank you for the brutal wake up calls and the newly found ability to see through other opportunists' crap.

The stories that follow are good or bad enough to become a very dramatic, long-running soap opera. This book is the story of my life and everything in it is true. Only the names have been changed to protect the guilty. I wrote this book to prove the naysayers wrong. To show the world that I overcame all the obstacles that were laid ahead of me. I didn't crumble. Similar to an over pressured clump of coal, I turned into a diamond. Furthermore, I want to give hope to those who are in need of it. Keep fighting, sufferers, keep reaching for the stars for, one day, you too will rid yourselves of the tribulations and come out victorious.

APARTMENT 10-D

Table of Contents

Bohio	7
Hyperthymesia	15
Champin	25
Regime Change	31
L'amour	37
Too Young	41
Moving Backwards	45
Babylon	57
No More Mister Nice Guy	69
Goldie	99
Boot Camp	107
Mississippi	115
Marriage	123
Leaving	141
About the Author	153

*"I promise, I will never treat others the way I was negatively treated;
it's bad enough I had to experience the maltreatment."*
-Verly E. Dolce

*"Only love, compassion, forgiveness and togetherness
can solve the world's complex problems, nothing else will do."*
-Verly E. Dolce

- Bohio -

My name is SonSonn. I was born in Bohio in 1985. Bohio is one of the three ancient names for the "Pearl" of the Caribbean islands, Ayiti Toma.

I had a deprived and abusive childhood, though I did not know it for the longest time. The lack of positive affirmations, food and love had taken a toll on me, and by the age of seventeen I weighed only 97 pounds fully dressed, the weight of an average American twelve-year-old.

I'll start by telling you a little more about my family dynamic. I am the third of several children from my sperm donor side. In this book, his name is Psychopath. He has, as far as I know, ten kids with six different mothers. His first five were with four different women.

My parents met when Psychopath, then a low-level member of the Haitian Army, was conducting a patrol of the city and its markets. The lack of a police force made the highly corrupt Army the sole provider of security and the only law enforcement agency. In typical fashion, Psychopath engaged in inappropriate relationships with the vendors he was supposed to protect. Psychopath noticed Surrogate, then a young woman, out on errands. He stepped in and worked his magic, the magic of romancing every woman possible, with no regrets. He told her the same lies he is still so good at communicating. She was too young and naïve to see through the smooth con artist.

Not long after they met, he tricked her into having to move in with him by keeping her out past her curfew, which forced her guardians to kick her out due to her disobedience.

Psychopath didn't tell Surrogate about his two children from two previous brief relationships until after they started living together. According to her, this was because he hadn't been comfortable enough to tell her sooner. Soon after sharing this news, he brought the children to live with them. This was in June of 1982.

I feel sure that Surrogate's frustration and rage stem from what Psychopath did to her from the beginning. He put her through hell — besides saddling her with his young children, he lied and cheated repeatedly, and did it all proudly.

The two kids were results of Psychopath's previous duty stations in the Haitian Army. Their mothers were from different parts of the country. My sister, Flight 191, was born in 1979 and my brother, Red October, in 1981. He was only eight months old when he came to live with Surrogate. Red October's mother lived, and still lives, in Gonaïves with her second family. I assume that if her socio-economic situation had been better she would not have given Red October up at such a young age, but then again, Psychopath — womanizer, con artist, fake charmer — may have promised her the world in exchange for her son. Or, he may have simply kidnapped my older brother outright — that sounds more like him, truthfully.

Flight 191 was nearly three years old when she arrived. The month before, her mother had a prophetic dream that accurately predicted her own death. Before taking that long journey of no return, she asked Surrogate to take care of her little girl. I'm told that Surrogate willingly took my sister in, (but didn't deliver on the promise made, in my opinion).

Surrogate often complained of her lack of preparation for responsibilities of this magnitude; she was only 20 years old when the kids arrived. Many times, she told tales of how she had to breastfeed Red October without lactation, since he was still of that age, and a mother-child bond was necessary. He had to endure withdrawal and separation symptoms that no child should ever experience.

In 1985, when I was born, it was the end of a political era for the country and the beginning of the ever-recurring nightmare that was my life. I was the lucky recipient of all of Surrogate's frustration, rage, hormonal imbalance and whatever else might have been involved.

In 1986, Psychopath came to the United States of America, shortly before my younger sister Forgetful was born. This would become a familiar pattern throughout our lives, abandoning his family and spreading his seeds around wherever he could find a woman who could bear him another child.

A sexual deviant and violent pedophile, he assaulted children as young as nine years old, even some of his own offspring. I wasn't one of those he sexually abused, but none of us grew up unscathed by him. Psychopath was abusive in many ways: emotionally, financially, psychologically. I carried much of the burden of his misdeeds and his deviant and devilish ways. I felt the guilt that should have been his.

I didn't really have a mother; I had a surrogate who, although she gave birth to me, denied I was hers, and treated me worse than the wicked stepmothers of fairy tales. She told me so often that I was adopted, I started to believe it. Her favorite threat to me was to send me to an orphanage. "I do not want you. You're not even my kid."

Almost daily, I looked forward to the day when I would be sent to this magical orphanage; I wanted it to happen so badly — but it never did.

I was such a bad kid that I would be sent to an orphanage. What did I do wrong? Absolutely nothing, besides bearing a strong resemblance to Psychopath. I looked like him and talked like him, and apparently I reasoned like him. Surrogate hated him; I resembled him, so she hated me. From as far back as I can remember, she terrorized me with threats of the many terrible things she would do to me, and often carried out her threats. Slavery-era-like tactics were used to humiliate, emasculate and control me. I would be walking along, minding my own business, and she'd suddenly hit me in the face or anywhere on my body with whatever object was close at hand.

She publicly humiliated and shamed me for the deficiencies she perceived in me: I was too short, too dark-skinned, my nose was too wide or not pointy enough. She claimed I was too dark to be hers, and the main reason my skin was so dark was because I didn't know how to shower properly; the darkness was nasty dirt that had been baked into my skin. She blamed my malnutrition on me. I was barely five feet tall for most of my teenage years. She blamed me for that as well. She said I ate enough and should have been taller than I was at the time. To acquire a more pointy nose, she ordered me to constantly pinch it while slowly running my thumb and index finger up and down along it to help reshape my nose to her desired shape.

I believed her. I adopted her image of me and became extremely insecure about my appearance. When I looked in the mirror, I saw what she saw: a short, ugly, too dark, too skinny, wide-nosed freak. I carried the shame well into adulthood. Because I never saw myself as a decent looking guy and had experienced only rejection, I would never approach women I thought were attractive; instead choosing homely partners.

I have the same skin complexion as Psychopath. I am taller than both of my parents and as for my nose, well, all the pinching and rubbing didn't change its shape. Scrubbing my skin did nothing to lighten it.

As I grew older, Surrogate's almost-daily beatings became more brutal. Most of them had a direct correlation with her feelings toward Psychopath. But sometimes they seemed to arise out of pure hatred for my existence. She would lock herself and me in a room and beat me until she could not go on any longer. The longest beating lasted well over three hours — with an occasional five-minute break to lower her blood pressure. This was one way she used to find joy, to beat me until it was medically unsafe for her to continue. I strongly believe she found her true happiness in beating me down until my body, soul and spirit were all broken.

Her favorite weapon was called an "Igwaz," a device many merchants used to whip livestock into obedience. The Igwaz was made of cow hide that had been braided and dried with a big piece of wood interwoven into the plaits. It was then tied up so it would be hard enough to inflict the most pain upon the animal. I often hid this devilish device of torture, but she always bought a new one fairly quickly because it was important to her to have one always ready and available, for either scheduled or impromptu whippings upon her worst creation, me. In the absence of her favorite mechanism of joy, she used anything she could find to get her fix. From a piece of two-by-four to an extension cord, to a rope used to tie up animals, or any other blunt object that could be used to inflict pain.

One time, Surrogate couldn't find anything suitable to beat me with, but needing the beating to make her happy for a short while, she grabbed a hand-held mirror and shattered it on my body — and then made me clean up the broken glass as punishment for breaking it.

Except for killing me, which she threatened to do many times, she did everything to me. She didn't only threaten to cut my tongue out, but once, she grabbed a straight razor and attempted to do so.

I had no safe place where unconditional love existed for me. No one in my family ever provided me with that space nor did they ever care enough to simply stop beating me while I was down.

When I was fourteen years old, my mother accused me of having lizard-like strong skin, because even after all the beatings and severe hits with blunt objects, I never showed any scars. Somehow, my body always healed in time for the next beating. This made her feel unaccomplished, which angered her so much that she became determined to mutilate my body via a major scar, one way or another. She told me that in those exact words.

From that point forward, instead of her usual non-stop and uncoordinated attacks, she focused on specific areas of my body with the sole purpose of finally achieving her long-awaited-dream, to permanently carve her hatred for me into my skin. Late that summer, she finally achieved nirvana. She hit me with the Igwaz so many times in my right biceps that the skin opened up like a clam shell, a gaping wound that for sure warranted proper medical care and stitches. I saw the many layers of skin ever so brightly because the gash was at least an inch deep into my skinny and weakened upper arm. I remember seeing the blood traveling up and down inside the mostly white veins/vessels. The arm was throbbing; I felt light-headed and almost fainted. She denied me medical treatment and refused to let me leave the house for at least one day, to ensure the wound would NOT heal properly and would therefore leave a scar. I still have the scar.

* * *

Over the years, my siblings came to live with us in stints. They were moved constantly; we never all stayed together for more than four years. The first time they were moved, they went to live at Psychopath's brother's house for a few years, and then at his father's house at L'acul-du-Nord in the countryside for another couple of years.

Red October is smart and a very nice guy, he really is. I was around five or six years old when I first realized this. Red October and Flight 191 had returned to live with us again. There were four of us kids, including my younger sister, Forgetful, the "favorite child." There was no way Surrogate was ever going to treat step-kids Red October and Flight 191 properly, as she was basically the epitome of the wicked stepmother. I was added to the list of step-kids by Surrogate, so now she had four kids living with her and only one was "hers." The other three were to be terrorized at every opportunity — and terrorizing she did.

When she came home from work at the end of the day, the very first thing she'd do (after giving us dirty looks), was to take Forgetful to whatever unoccupied room she could find for their daily "conference." The conference involved Forgetful regurgitating all the dirt she had accumulated that day on her siblings. She would snitch on us, telling Surrogate everything that had happened that day, sometimes including incidents she'd forgotten to tell her on previous days. Then the three of us would have to line up for extremely violent beatings. One by one we would get pummeled by Surrogate, with any objects she could find to throw at us or beat us with. There was no reasoning with her. She was an authoritarian dictator with her own sociopathic tendencies, and she was basically using us as a way to get rid of all her frustrations in life.

She had a lot of tension. Even without Psychopath, life in Bohio was never easy. There were too many of us and never enough food. Surrogate's job as a housekeeper for supposedly rich people (people who either act rich or think they're rich) cleaning their toilets and houses, was extremely low paying. I don't believe she made more than two hundred and fifty U.S. dollars per year. It might have been even less, but no matter how little she made, at least ten percent of whatever she earned had to be tithed to the church — that was a requirement she would not miss for the world. A couple of times we nearly died of hunger because the church money wasn't to be touched. The church's power over Surrogate was so great that she was willing to let herself and her kids die of hunger in order to please a pastor who I highly doubt even remembered her name. Or to please a white God and his white son, Jesus H. Christ, whose very image surfaced only around 500 years ago.

Most of the dysfunction in our family centered around one person, Psychopath. Psychopath loved to create weird family dynamics and force people into situations where they had to get along together. He loved putting people together — not while he was there or had any ability to keep the relationships beneficial for all involved. He orchestrated the moves of my siblings from afar most of the time. From what I hear, he still enjoys creating complex problems that he alone can fix to get the credit and feel like a hero of some sort. He is no hero, he's anything but.

Recently, Red October told me that Psychopath is still unremorseful for all the chaos he created, and acts like he is the victim in the very scenarios he rendered so unpleasant for all.

Flight 191 shared some of the unfortunate traits of Psychopath; however, as a female, maybe she should have been a little bit more conservative for her own sake. But that wasn't her way. She was a good person although she had some questionable friends. She became pregnant as a teenager but didn't let that stop her from pursuing her education shortly after giving birth. She was just all about it, living life to the fullest — and she lived and died the way she wanted. Airline Flight 191 ended in a hot fiery crash in Chicago (a few miles away from the airport) and all aboard perished. My sister's life went up and down similarly. She was 26 years old in 2006 when she passed away due to a long-endured illness. I hope she's in a much better place now and she's no longer suffering from the terrible genes that were passed down to us from the "wonderful" man named Psychopath.

VERLY E. DOLCE

My father never helped me with the guilt I bore for him. Instead, he added to it by accusing me of being a bad kid and stealing money from him, and for making him believe that I would be the one kid who was going to help him out and really have his back, and then letting him down. In reality, I did have his back. But regardless of anything I ever did for him, the extreme measures I took to be there for this man, it was never enough — because after all, his name is Psychopath, and that's how psychopaths are.

When I eventually started talking to the few people I was allowed contact with, I began to realize that I just might be living a very crappy life. Somehow I had been making it work, but the truth was my loveless and hunger-filled existence was a constant nightmare, both literally and figuratively. I was prone to sleepwalking, at least five nights a week. Not ironically, the episodes often involved me attempting to leave the house in the middle of the night. Surrogate always caught me. She proudly proclaimed that she often had to beat me down in order to prevent my subconscious from trying to escape from my real-life nightmare. The sleepwalking occurrences often triggered bed-wetting. I unfortunately wet the bed constantly until I was about sixteen years old. She blamed me for not dealing well with the toxic environment she created for me. She often accused me of being weak and of being the Devil's spawn.

Surrogate felt no remorse for her lack of care or affection towards me, her first kid, her only son. Even to this day, she shows no remorse. She doesn't regret anything she did and somehow justifies all of her actions, regardless of how terrible they were.

Positive affirmations that have the potential to turn a young man into a useful member of society were never uttered by anyone — except one person, my Grandma Rose. My grandmother made living with Surrogate not as terrible as it could have been. She saw in me what her own child, Surrogate, refused or failed to see. She was often my savior, somehow sensing when I needed her at the worst of times, arriving unexpectedly to bring rescue and reprieve. My grandma defended me against Surrogate, even threatening her: "Don't you ever beat on him again in my presence! If I ever catch you doing it, I will beat you down worse than you did him." I believed it. We all did. She meant it. She continued, "If I had treated you the way you treat him, you wouldn't be the woman you are today." She closed with, "He is a special boy who will do great things; mark my words, you'll regret treating him like that soon enough."

Grandma and I, we connected on a telepathic level. Often I would receive a telepathic message to alert me of her potential visit ahead of her arrival. I knew more about her life than any other grandkid did and she knew me better than anyone else, including the woman who'd supposedly pushed me out her loins.

When I was very young, she gave me the nickname "SonSonn." I don't know where she got it, but for as long as I can remember that was the name most people called me. None of my cousins got a cool nickname from her.

During summer vacations, she often woke me in the middle of the night to check on me, but she did it so tenderly, I would fall right back to sleep and often dreamt of the scenario as being magical. I loved her; she loved me. We trusted each other with our lives. Rose made me feel like a KING. She talked to me like I was the most important person in her life, and I reciprocated that feeling. She is the GREATEST person who ever lived, in my opinion. She was and will forever be my knight in shining armour.

I loved when she would tell me stories of her life. This extraordinary woman had given birth, at home, to 13 children, including three sets of twins, with no epidurals and no trained OB-GYN or nurse present. With only the help of a Doula, she endured labor like the champion she was.

Grandma and I always gave each other gifts when we saw one another. She never had me measured for articles of clothing but somehow, knew my exact size from birth to seventeen years old. Whenever she brought me a piece of clothing, it fit as if I'd had it tailored for me. I always made sure I had some money to buy her food when she visited. I could go days or weeks without ever touching a penny until the day she was to come by. The universe ALWAYS blessed me with enough to take care of my grandma's hunger.

Most of my siblings never realized she gave any presents because she didn't always bring one for them. She would sneak me the gifts once the other kids went to play or moved out of sight.

She lived deep in the countryside so her visits always started in the morning. She had to walk for at least 10 miles to get to downtown L'acul-du-Nord. From there, she would endeavor to see as many of her kids as possible. She would miss one or two grandkids here and there but she never missed seeing her favorite grandkid, me. I always knew she was coming; a feeling of invincibility would overpower me and bring with it the strongest feeling of joy I've ever experienced. As soon as this feeling started, I would make my way home to greet my favorite person ever.

I never left her side. I would buy her food, get clean water for her to drink or for washing up, and she and I would chat for hours.

Grandma Rose didn't need material things like expensive furniture or clothes. Conveniences such as running water, proper plumbing or electricity were absent from her life. She never owned a cell phone. She never left Bohio and had no formal education, if any. She had the one thing that trumped all of that. She had enough love in her heart to give to the entire world and still have some left over for future generations. She knew how to make people feel valued. She made me feel big. Not big in terms of weight, but big like I could accomplish anything and no obstacle was too large to stop me from becoming anything I wanted to.

When I would visit her in Laplange, she'd constantly give me praise, as if she could see that my soul was severely depleted from living with abusers.

During the summer of 1998, we all went there on vacation. Grandma was cooking for us in the makeshift kitchen. The kitchen was simply made: four pieces of wood in the ground, connected on top and covered with dried palm tree leaves. The "oven" consisted of three solid rocks placed in a triangular position, and the wood would be fed through them to cook. To kill the heat, the wood would be displaced or pulled back.

Some of the kids were eating ripe mangoes, and ran off to play, leaving a huge mess of mango skins and trash all over. My grandfather, Grandma Rose's husband of over thirty years, came out and started yelling and cussing at me. Grandma came running from the kitchen, charging at my grandfather. She raised her voice above his and went to town. She told him to never dare talk to me that way. She said some very strong words to her own husband in my defense. He called me a little pig. She called him a bigger pig who should go rub his nose on a pile of wet horse doo doo if he had the intention to ever talk to me like that.

I don't know if Grandma saw the other kids making the mess, but she knew I would never do something so foolish or careless. She was certain I wasn't the culprit. She knew me better, back then, than I know myself today.

I was stunned. I was speechless. I saw that this woman defended me and put me above her own marital vows to my grandfather. Right then I knew that no matter what, she had my back for life.

- Hyperthymesia -

From a very young age, I sensed I was different from the rest of my family, although nothing was ever said about it. It was partly my ability to remember incidents that happened very early in my life. I remember a tricycle with a lot of colors and big black plastic tires. The handlebars and seat were blue; the body was mostly red, and there were some accents of yellow somewhere on it. I remember the neighbor women teasing me when they'd see me riding my tricycle. They'd call out to me that I was their boyfriend. This seemed to be a customary form of teasing in Bohio, but, somehow I took them seriously and really believed them.

Late one afternoon I was playing on the porch with my back toward the front door. The tricycle was on my left with the wheels facing the living room window. Red October came out and hopped onto it and started pedaling, but before he could reach the end of the porch, there was a loud crack and thump that startled me. At six years old, his weight was too much for my toddler bike and it broke. I was too young to understand what had happened so I didn't pay too much attention to the commotion going on inside the house. Surrogate had called Red October inside and was yelling at him because Surrogate, never known to be subtle or understanding, was furious at him for breaking my tricycle. This happened at the end of summer in 1987.

A few years ago, in 2017, I told Surrogate what I remembered of this story. She was amazed that I had any memory of the incident. She told me "You'd just turned two; we got you the tricycle and then Red October broke it."

Another story I recall vividly, like it happened yesterday, was my little cousin Sindine being born. We were at my Grandma Rose's house, and Surrogate's little sister Ana was in labor, about to give birth. I heard what was probably the loudest scream I'd ever heard and I rushed over to Ana. She must have been between contractions because she was calmly eating some bread. I loved that bread and I wanted some. It was really good bread that we called

Pain Gouden from the small bakery across the street. A small segment of a loaf cost only a nickel back in those days. There were four segments in her left hand, and to my two-year-old eyes they looked massive and irresistible. She also had some coffee that looked good, they wouldn't give me any, saying I was too young. I disagreed. I felt I deserved coffee and bread because everyone else had some. I grabbed the bread and coffee cup out of her hands and ran and hid behind the house where I enjoyed the crap out of that bread and coffee. A short time later I heard a baby crying.

When I told Surrogate that story recently, she was again amazed. "That's crazy. How could you remember that story? You had just turned two years old!"

* * *

Starting in 1989, I started to hear rumors of Sindine's father, The Prophet, being an undercover homosexual. An extremely light-skinned man of average height and build, he was a well-known Catholic cleric with deep ties in the community. People talked openly about his sexuality in front of me, perhaps thinking I wouldn't comprehend what they were saying. I did. Regardless of the rumors, he was thought of as a nice man and was well-respected by all. I used to go say hi to him whenever I went to L'acul-du-Nord to visit my grandma and the others and he always gave me at least five Gourdes every time I went to say hi to him.

I adored my Aunty Ana, who was very loving, sweet and generous. I often felt she should have been my mother. Not because I didn't have a mother, but because of the contrast between her and Surrogate. An incident I witnessed in the summer of 1995 really affected me. Ana came home from work one evening and my cousin Sindine wasn't home. That wasn't the case usually. Ana became very worried and went house to house searching for her. She enlisted my help in the search, and we finally found Sindine at her friend Carole's house, which was right outside of the tiny cul-de-sac where we had once lived. Although relieved her daughter was found safe, Aunt Ana was so upset that she hit Sindine. Right away, Ana burst into tears, crying uncontrollably and apologizing to my cousin for what she had done. When I saw her crying and asking her child for forgiveness, I understood that she found no pleasure in inflicting pain upon the body of someone she loved so dearly. This was a true loving and caring mother. Surrogate's style of motherhood was the complete opposite of Aunt Ana's.

* * *

The bakery was a special place to me because it helped create a meaningful bond between me and my first-ever favorite person, Grandma Rose's first kid, Uncle Golden Child. He was an avid soccer player, he played semi-professionally for many years. Uncle Golden Child adored me and I him. He showed me what the love of a family should feel like. Before he went to work, he always left money with someone else to buy me bread when I woke up. My admiration for my uncle is not so much because he left money for others to buy me bread at the bakery. It was because his love for me was ever present. He took me everywhere in his pick-up truck. On his days off, he would take me on long drives, just the two of us. I felt he knew me. The real me. Way before I found out who I was. As if Uncle Golden Child had premonitions of the future and he knew I would set out to help the world one day. He loved hanging out with me. He took me around to his colleagues and friends to show off my superior spelling abilities. He set out to prove that none of the neighborhood kids could defeat me in spelling, mathematics or analytical thinking. Even the ones who were many grades above me were no match.

Sadly, Uncle Golden Child was taken away from us way too early, he was gone before I turned nine years old. They presumed I was too young to tell me what transpired. I understood it all. I understood more than they gave me credit for. It is widely believed in my family that the parents of one of his suitors invoked the negative powers of the world of Voodoo to strike him down. They selfishly came for his life, and they got it. He was chased down by a piece of tin roof in broad daylight by a sudden unusual hurricane-like wind that was far too powerful for a tropical climate. My grandma never made an effort to find out who the culprits were because she believed in love more than revenge. We had our suspicions because the town wasn't that big and people talked.

Grandma Rose was never the same after he was taken from us. For the rest of her life, she couldn't look at a picture of him without bursting into agonized tears. The thought of him brought her down to the floor. I felt her sorrow when she spoke of him, or if someone simply mentioned his name. I always consoled her because he meant the world to me also. She and I, we also shared that tremendous loss. The sole picture of my uncle that was in existence near her was a photo of him with his soccer team in full uniform. That picture had to be shared in secret, covertly to prevent Grandma from seeing or hearing about it. The pain was too much for her to bear. Knowing Surrogate and the others a little better, I sympathize more with my grandma; the others DON'T measure up to him. They are all ok individuals with some minor exceptions. He was a kind, fun-loving person. The glue that kept the family together.

I say the bakery was very special to me because it was the only reminder of Uncle Golden that wasn't hidden or destroyed to prevent my grandma's early demise due to heartache. It wasn't just a wood-fired oven covered in mud. It was the center of the special bond between an uncle and his nephew. Whenever I went to visit, I often felt an urge to walk by the old oven. I went out of my way at times to go there. Sometimes, I did so subconsciously. It wasn't until I arrived at my destination that it would hit me. Muscle memory, I guess. Or maybe it was because his presence could still be felt there and I needed that lift to my spirit and self-esteem. To most people it was an old oven that was no longer functioning. To me, it was a place of joy. A place of lasting joyous memories and sustained camaraderie. It was as if he was smiling at me. It was and still is in my heart. I have yet to duplicate the feeling that overpowered me when we were together. I felt important. I felt like I was somebody and I always would be somebody important to at least one person. He knew how to show his appreciation for other humans, especially his favorite nephew, ME! Only when I would visit my grandma would my sense of belonging return. That feeling of being loved and adored overshadowed my entire visit. Every visit.

The bakery was NOT built by professionals, it was home-made. The main heat source was chopped up wood packed very tightly to create the higher than average temperatures needed for the bread to rise and the walls were made of brick covered with mud to prevent heat from escaping.

Most of the time, my uncle would hold my hand when we crossed the street and arrived at **GOODIES TOWN**. I had food for days, it seemed. It didn't take a lot to make me happy. Even today, it doesn't take a lot to make me happy, and I feel the very early connection I shared with my grandma and uncle are partly responsible for my outgoing nature and simple way of living.

* * *

As a child in Bohio, I slept on the cold dirt or cheaply paved cement floor. I didn't start sleeping regularly on a bed with a mattress until the summer of 2001 when I was fifteen. When I was ten years old, while asleep one the floor, rats ate the bottoms of both of my feet. They nibbled away what felt like a quarter inch of my plantar. There was some bleeding and the pain was unbearable. It was impossible for me to walk, stand or do simple tasks, but I was ordered to walk to school by Surrogate. I did somehow. I had to or else.

This event was largely caused by the absence of our cat, Mina, who was great at scaring away the mice and rats who dared enter our house. Most days, she turned her catch into snacks. Mina was black and white with the lighter coloring mostly on her paws and underbelly. She was very smart, attentive and loyal. Mina was killed for her meat by our neighbor. He shared his secret with another neighbor, telling her how he turned our cat into a pot of stew and ate like a king that day. His secret-keeper told Surrogate the story a few months after we stopped looking for Mina. It still breaks my heart when her memory comes to my mind. She was my best friend. There's a photo of me with her at Red October's first communion in 1993. Surrogate has that picture.

We rarely had enough money to purchase meat, but whenever we did, we would buy a chicken for Sunday after-church dinner. Surrogate would go get it on Thursday or Friday. Sometimes she would send Flight 191 or occasionally, Red October.

Our combination backyard, hallway and kitchen was a very tiny space, no more than three feet wide and ten feet long. When the chicken was brought home, it would be tied by a leg to a cement block and ignored by everyone except me. I would play with it and feed it and make friends with it. Then on Sunday when they came to kill it, it always hurt me. It wasn't solely the way they would kill it, but the manner they did it. One of them would walk up to the chicken and grab its head real quick and chop at its neck with a sharp knife. Then they'd shove a big pot over the dying bird, stepping on it to hold it down. The chicken would struggle for a while, suffering. Finally, it would stop moving, leaving a trail of blood oozing from under the pot. They'd have another pot of lukewarm water ready, that wouldn't thoroughly cook the meat. One of them, usually Flight 191 or Surrogate, would take the chicken's lifeless body and plunge it in and lift it out again. That would loosen up the skin so the feathers could be plucked much faster and more efficiently. After plucking out the feathers, they would inspect it and clean it again. They would cut the head off and get rid of it, and then finish preparing the chicken.

With no stove, oven or barbecue, we didn't have any way of browning the skin. They'd wrap it in newspaper and lightly run it over an open fire. They'd use "Charbon," a coal-like substance made from wood brought down from the mountains. It wasn't real coal; it was wood burned to look like coal and also have the same consistency. To make Charbon, trees were cut down and the wood neatly stacked in a high pile with highly combustible materials at the base of the pile. Dried leaves were added on top to help seal the "air vents." When it was mostly sealed, wet dirt or hard mud was packed on to make it really condensed. A small hole was left so that when it was fired up, the mud on the outside would prevent the fire on the inside from fully materializing. Streams of thick white smoke would escape through the mud. The wood never burned to ash because it was mostly being suffocated. It would turn a coal-like color but maintain the consistency of wood — though a much drier and highly combustible piece of wood that cracked as it was being burned for the second time.

After it cooled overnight, merchants would open up the dome-like pile of dirt to disclose the mostly burned wood that had somehow kept its shape during the slow burn. They'd fill big sacks with the Charbon. Empty 50- or 100-pound rice bags imported from the U.S. were ideal for this purpose. Number 10 metal cans were used as a unit of measurement for this environmentally devastating product, that is somehow necessary for the survival of some of the country's poor and underserved families. The production of this fuel source is directly related to deforestation, catastrophic floods and many other major environmental issues faced by the country of Bohio. Future generations will also suffer because of it. The canister, or mamit, full of this coal substitute is still being sold in open air markets all over the country and remains the primary source of cooking fuel for most of the population. There are some alternatives in the market presently but their high cost and lack of viability is still a major concern for poor Haitians.

Most Sundays, Flight 191 was in charge of the cooking. She would build a really hot fire, cover the chicken with old newspapers and then lightly run it over the fire. The newspaper was thin and burned easily, and when it burned, it created a thin white smoke that didn't really cook the chicken, but turned it a golden-brown color. That is how she would flambé our chicken on Sunday whenever we'd had enough money to buy one three days earlier. This was a regular occurrence for at least three or four years. I would watch the whole procedure, first because I was very inquisitive, and also because I wanted to know what happened to my friend.

I usually refused to eat the chicken. And, of course, when I declined to eat it, I'd be beaten by Surrogate or hit in the head by Flight 191. Somebody would always call me ungrateful or say I didn't understand life, and they'd ask, "What is wrong with you?!" But I always stood firm. Why wouldn't I do it? It was not because I was vegan or vegetarian. I felt that the way chickens were treated, the way animals in general were being mistreated in the country, was unfair and inhumane. "I'm not doing it," I would say. "I'm not doing it because it doesn't make any sense."

- Champin -

We moved often during the following years: from Port-au-Prince to L'acul-du-Nord and then to Champin at the beginning of 1990. The pick-up truck we'd chartered for the Champin move dropped us off at the entrance of carrefour Champin, across from Hotel Sainte Philomene and the Baptist Church that Surrogate would soon frequent.

Our very first night in the house we did not have any doors, but we were all too tired to care. We put barely anything in front of the door openings and went to bed, leaving the door problem for the next day.

Our landlord's name was Salnave. Some people didn't have a lot of good things to say about him, but as far as I know he was an okay guy.

During the years of 1991 to 1993, Surrogate suffered several seizures, sometimes causing her to pass out. I don't know the cause of these medical emergencies, but she was never taken to the hospital during or after they occurred. The episodes would start with her becoming extremely stiff and rocking back and forth, without the ability to speak. The adults would procure a metal spoon and use the handle to pry open her mouth to prevent her teeth from grinding. They always reminded one another NOT to let their fingers get between her teeth in the process. They washed her face in cold water and monitored her vital signs throughout the episode, making sure she came to. It was very scary for me, especially once when she was foaming at the mouth.

Surrogate had a love interest for a time, Ivan. He was an auto mechanic who specialized in every type of motor vehicle that was in the country at the time. Ivan was, and might still be, an extremely talented mechanic. He worked on everything from 18-wheelers and big school buses to tiny sedans. The school buses that were mostly imported were Blue Bird, the big blue ones.

The relationship between Surrogate and Ivan happened as a result of Psychopath having a new person of interest in Babylon therefore, he couldn't take care of us, his other family in Bohio. Being a one-family-at-a-time kind of guy, the minute he moved on to a new family, previous ones were forgotten. Perhaps he'd already had prospects lined up when he landed at Miami International Airport. In any case, by 1993 he had completely abandoned us and moved in with a much older woman, The Cougar. They soon had a kid together and he officially discarded us like hot stinky garbage. The fresh new kid and the new relationship became his world.

Besides being talented, Ivan was a nice guy. His garage was across the street from us but he lived far away. Not long after he and Surrogate met, they progressed from friendly neighbor chit-chats to lovers' trysts. Ivan was very generous and treated all of us better than Psychopath ever had. He had a son, Boulon, a joyful and chubby boy a year younger than me. Boulon moved in with us within a year of the start of their relationship. I believe Boulon was a nickname, because other overweight people were nicknamed that back then.

Ivan had a fairly recent Volvo. It was beige with leather interior, a very nice and recent four-door sedan. A couple of times when I heard him say he was going somewhere, I would stow away on the floor behind the front seat. When he got to his destination and found me, he never yelled or did anything bad to me. I did this once when he went to Odikap. This was a place by the river where people would get their cars washed. Instead of traditional car washing places, people would take their cars to a very shallow river and young boys (often miscreants or orphans who didn't go to school) would wash their cars for spare change.

Ivan and Surrogate's relationship ended after Psychopath's mother came to visit unannounced in 1993. She noticed Ivan's kid in the house and informed Psychopath that Surrogate had moved on and was in a new relationship. Within months, Psychopath unashamedly came back into our lives to destroy what he hadn't had a hand in building. He beat Surrogate until her eyes bled; he chased Flight 191 with a very sharp knife and he "whupped" everyone else in his path. Regrettably, he conned me into being his informant by manipulating me with his favorite brand of lies; "You know you're my favorite kid, right?" Is the exact sentence he uttered to me back then.

At that time, Surrogate's marathon beatings were becoming more and more frequent; often more than two hours of nonstop beating for no reason whatsoever. While pummeling me, she kept yelling about how I reminded her of my father and how much she hated him. Once she beat me for being in third place in my class academically, loudly proclaiming, "You need to come in first place!" I ranked third. That wasn't good enough. She has yet to help me with a single school assignment. After being in the U.S. for nearly ten years, she is still unable to complete a simple form without any issues. I'm just saying… With her, it is, Do as I say, not as I do.

Needless to say, Psychopath caught me at a very vulnerable time. Surrogate had shown me how much she hated me, and this con artist came in at the right moment to ask me for valuable information. I gave it to him. He used the information extorted from a seven-year-old to terrorize everyone, including me, the informant.

That same month, Surrogate asked this loser to marry her under an old alias he hadn't used in almost a decade. He couldn't marry her using his real name because he was already married in the U.S. to the Cougar. Her eyes still had leftover blood from when he'd punched her not even two weeks earlier. Why did she want to be married so badly? Simply because she wanted to be more involved in the nearby church and needed wife status. Psychopath agreed to marry her under the alias, which didn't appear on any other official documents. Nine months after this sham wedding, in November 1994, the twins were born.

This was around the time I first realized I was able to walk to school by myself. I was in first grade, and it was approaching time for me to go, but nobody was available to walk me there. Even though we were dirt poor, somehow we could afford the services of a maid, and our maid, T-Dane, would walk me to school every day. On the way, she'd tell me stories of her old life and how she would one day be doing better financially. I listened carefully because she was so nice to me. Due to illness, she couldn't come to work that fateful Monday morning. Everybody was baffled about what to do because everyone had somewhere to go, and they were all going in the wrong direction. It would be a major inconvenience for anyone to walk me to school.

I spoke up. I said, "I can walk to school by myself — I don't need no help."

I'm sure it was a little odd for them to hear that from a seven-year-old, considering the school was several miles away, roughly an hour's walk.

I walked to school, and when school got out that afternoon, I gathered my things and walked back home. Everyone was amazed. Kids in third and fourth grade still needed companions and buddies to go across the street, but I went all the way to school without any help. After that, I always went to school by myself, and within three years, I also started walking my little sister to school. Her kindergarten, College Anne-Marie Obas, was directly across from my primary-middle school, Foundation President Stenio Vincent, Freres Salesiens de Don Bosco.

I never got lost. Not one time. I was never scared to make the trip, ever. I felt as if it was long overdue. I felt like they had shown me the way once and it was my time to prove that I knew how to do it. The many other times someone had walked me to school, I'd felt it was unnecessary and uncalled for. I thought they ought to trust in my ability to do things on my own.

I learned from my uncle Sam, who was in high school at the time, how to tell directions using the Sun as my guide. Sam was staying with us at the time, and he and his classmates often discussed their weekly lessons in my presence. They used to work on most subjects, and I tried to pay attention and retain whatever they talked about because I knew it would come in handy one day. From his studying, their hot philosophical debates, and what I retained, I figured that as long as I knew where the Sun was, I could correctly identify my East and West and the rest would be a piece of cake. And it was.

Often, grown folks did a double take as I walked past them. I didn't know why they kept staring at me. I thought it was strange. At a very young age, I knew everything needed to navigate the city safely. I knew my numbers, letters, colors and how to get home by foot from most places. It wasn't that hard, in my opinion.

In 2020, I remain astonished whenever I hear the following from anyone, especially an adult: "I'm NOT GOOD with directions." It amazes and scares me at the same time to hear those words come out of another human being's lips, especially if the individual is more than ten years old. That is absurd, unreal, downright wrong. For millennia, humans have utilized their intellect and knowledge of basic astronomy to navigate and circumvent the globe. We have survived as a species due to our abilities to adapt and adjust to our environment. Today, there are tools available that many of our predecessors couldn't imagine or would have died to have. But somehow, people are repeating this moronic statement.

I was always the youngest, smallest and shortest in all my classes. The teachers loved me and so did the school principal, Madame Daniel. At school I was treated with respect and compassion, the opposite of my home environment. The education I received at that school is unmatched by anywhere else I have been since. I had an inquisitive mind and they filled it up with enough knowledge to keep me busy and entertained.

- Regime Change -

Papa Doc ruled Bohio from 1957 until his death in 1971, when his son, Baby Doc, took over as the new dictator at nineteen years old. During their rule, both men referred to themselves as "President for life." They were each given the green light by the U.S. Government because they were extremely pro-American.

The son became "dictator for life," however, he was incompetent, not ready, not experienced, had no clue what the heck was going on. He was a rich, idiotic, fat kid who had no political experience and was behind a military who obviously didn't like him very much. Why else would they overthrow him? Which they did.

In 1986, a coup d'état took place, ending the regime of Baby Doc and running him out of the country. He went into exile in France where he remained until the first "technically" legal Presidential elections of 1990 and subsequent inauguration on February 7, 1991.

During my childhood there were many different governments, a lot of changes. No regime lasted even two years. I remember seeing Haitian soldiers of different regimes and ranks driving around. The vehicles were similar but the uniforms were different. Some were all green, others had navy blue pants and light blue shirts. I was too young to make sense of what was happening around me.

There were many regions where one group of people was totally pro-government and willing to die for it, while another group hated the first group and was murdering people left and right. There were people killing each other over political ideologies that none of us really understood. There was no U.S. intervention, at least not on paper — but we all know better than that. The U.S. government had been using intelligence and counterintelligence (such as the FBI's COINTELPRO, and the CIA's clandestine services) to facilitate the effective destabilization of that country ever since its inception.

We didn't know who was really controlling the situation. We didn't know who was really in charge of the economy. We didn't know who was really in charge of the government. It was difficult to find out because there were few sources of information. Televisions were scarce and our family was too poor to afford one, except for a small 19-inch black and white TV that didn't have an antenna good enough to receive many channels.

February 7, 1991 was our second independence. That's what they called it. We had a new president, and his name was Jean-Bertrand Aristide, also known as The Priest or Little Priest. Aristide gave up the priesthood to marry a woman who had worked for the U.S. government, and then he became a political activist and leader of the political party he founded, "Fanmi Lavalas." Members of Fanmi Lavalas had participated in the coup to overthrow the previous government of Baby Doc. The party is still active in Bohio, and among the overly-loyal Haitian diaspora. One of my closest friends is still a die-hard member of their Boston chapter.

Obviously it had been a marginally corrupted election, Aristide won the presidency by a landslide because he ran on a platform that government officials should be elected by the people, for the people. Unhindered and popular democracy. One reason so many people were behind him was because he was the president of the people. He went to homeless shelters and ate with the poor. He would visit different schools and sit down with students and share a meal with them. He'd go into the streets, and he didn't really have much more security than anyone else. He was really engaged, so everybody supposedly voted for him, but then he got exiled. He never did half of his term. He was elected twice: first in 1990-'91 and then again in 2000-'01. He was exiled then also.

He was the president and political leader of the people, but the wrong people. He was the president of the masses and the common folk, but not necessarily of those with controlling interests in companies that were operating in Bohio. Nor did he understand (or maybe he did and didn't care) that if you don't go with those people, you don't go with their rhetoric, you don't go with their ideologies, if you go against them, or you're trying to overtax them, "they" will overthrow your entire government and send you into exile to a place you never heard of and wouldn't want to live. That's what "they" did to Aristide, twice. "They" are the conglomerates, foreign entities and nations with vested interests in the country.

I'm not saying that I preferred him one way or another; I'm just saying that he must have overstepped somewhere, made good on too many promises to the general population, and whomever was in charge, those people who are still in charge of the world, that we don't even know about, they clearly did not like that. And they took care of it. They took care of him.

So around 1991, after the first coup d'état happened, again there were different regime changes and military juntas in which some generals came together and put themselves in power. In the midst of the political turmoil and confusion, we had more than three different administrations. They ranged from military juntas to random military generals declaring themselves president and everything in between.

A little-known fact about that time span is that Ertha Pascal-Trouillot became Haiti's and North America's first female president (Haiti is on the North American plate). She was the leader of the provisional government for eleven months. She turned over the Presidential Sash to the Priest on February 7th, 1991.

One specific moment stood out for me. Right after Aristide left power, the military took over again and they were doing their own thing. All the police outposts were persecuting people because the government really wasn't into anti-government rallies or any kind of association that was perceived as anti-government, both under the Papa Doc and Baby Doc regimes. The corruption was at an all-time high. It is somehow worse today than it was then. No one could have predicted that.

Once, in January of 1991, I witnessed a dysfunctional trial in Champin at the nearby police outpost. The country didn't yet have a police force, it wasn't established until after the 1991 Presidential inauguration. The police station was across from the church, down about half a mile on the right side, and across the big open canal where the water flowed ever so slowly due to debris. Red October and I came upon it and we stopped to watch. Everything that was happening was in plain view because the fencing was mostly steel bars and there were two or three offices. We could stand outside and hold onto the bars and watch what was going on inside.

The accused man was tied up like a hog. His hands and feet were tied behind him, and they had joined his hands and his feet together so he was bent to resemble a triangle. Obviously, being tied up like that was painful, and he was crying on the floor. Whoever was in charge read the charges against him. He was accused of stealing. I don't believe the person who accused him was even there, so he didn't even have the right to face his accuser. At the very least, he should have had a lawyer, but he didn't appear to have any representation or anybody there for him. After reading the charges, the man announced, "You've been found guilty." And he started beating him mercilessly. The prisoner couldn't even say a word to defend himself.

I started crying. I thought to myself; Why were they beating this guy so senselessly like he'd committed a capital crime? Something truly horrible? He didn't do that. He was accused of stealing something. That's it.

Red October looked at me. He smacked me in the back of the head and said, "What is wrong with you?"

I told him, "This doesn't make sense. If he really did it, how come they don't let him speak?" "Hear him out"

And then he hit me again and said, "Is he your father or something? Why do you feel bad for him?"

At that point I had to wipe my tears, and Red October grabbed my hand and we walked back home, which wasn't very far. I felt kind of strange. I wondered why I was so upset that this guy didn't get a fair trial.

He didn't because the outpost wasn't a court of law. Those were very scarce. There were only a few of them in the entire region of the North or North-Central, where we lived. There were more police stations and prisons.

A lot of those. This guy wasn't in the court system. He was in the police station, being judged by army officers or whatever, and then they proceeded to beat the crap out of him. He was bleeding and everybody was chanting. It didn't make sense to me then. It still doesn't make sense, and I'm still against it, but back then it hit me and I thought: Something doesn't add up.

- L'amour -

After Champin, we moved into another house, in Site Chovèl. Things were a little different there. Psychopath, continuing his pattern of reappearing every so often, had reengaged with us. He came down in 1992, right after we moved there, and he even helped out a couple of times.

Another of Surrogate's sisters, Carmen, had met the man of her dreams and was to be married. At that time they were both young but they're still married today. I was going to be the ring bearer at their wedding, because I guess that's what they do with cute kids. At seven years old, I already understood the sense of logically framing a conversation to make my point with Psychopath if I wanted his help. I asked him, "Would you please help me get my ring bearer's outfit?" I was prepared to present my carefully considered strategic arguments but he simply replied, "I'll help you."

He bought me the outfit: thick black wool pants, a salmon shirt surrounded by frills on both sides of the buttons, a black cummerbund and a bow tie. The ceremony took place at an out-of-the-way but historic church in Vaudreuil right off the Route Nationale #1, not far from where the American missionaries had their free clinic once a week, and near the campus of the Christian Radio station 4VEH, 94.1-FM.

I proudly carried the ring, and I still remember the entire event. I had to walk up the aisle carrying a little satin pillow with the ring attached. The wedding give-away gift to the ring bearer was a porcelain figurine, a mostly white, winged, female angel that was shiny and sought after. Unfortunately, I accidentally dropped it after the ceremony, causing Surrogate to do to me what she knew and loved best — yelling and screaming that, as always, led to physical abuse. Her favorite way of conveying her back-asswards messages.

At that time, Carmen had only one child, her daughter, Vanoue, from a previous relationship that didn't work out. Vanoue was born around the same time as Sindine. I don't remember her birth, but I do recall seeing her as a tiny baby at Grandma's house shortly after. Vanoue is my closest cousin and she and I remain close to this day. She has recently moved to the Bahamas with her new husband.

Aunt Carmen and I, we share a special unbreakable bond. She understands me and I her. Even if we go for years without speaking or seeing one another, at our next meeting, it always feels like we saw one another the day before. She's part of a rare breed of women, the type of person who can uplift me by simply seeing their faces or by thinking about them. That's my Auntie Carmen. She makes me feel special and treats me like I'm her own son. She tells everyone that I am her first kid. She never calls me by name, but rather, "my son." She has two boys but she reminds them often that I'm to be respected and regarded as their older brother.

Carmen was the first person I ever made a real grown-up promise to. The summer of 1997 she came to visit us in bas-de-Vertieres. I was almost twelve years old. I told her these exact words: "Everything I have or ever will have, I will always share with you." I meant what I said.

In 2009, I went back to Bohio for the first time since moving to the U.S. On my third day there, Surrogate's presence at Uncle Sam's house was a bit too much to bear; I had a piercing headache and I couldn't stand her presence for another second. She couldn't take it either; she left the house, but my headache stayed. Within minutes, Auntie Carmen walked through the door and, like magic, the headache dissolved. I felt immense joy overcoming me. I jumped up, hugged her like my life depended on it, and then I had a sudden urge to go buy her something to eat. Something kept telling me to do it. I used to get these same intuitions whenever my grandma would visit.

We walked down to the nearest street vendor and on our way, she asked me, "How did you know I was starving?" I simply smiled, because she and I both know our connection transcends the conventional or quantitative realms and is more metaphysical.

- Too Young -

Shortly after Carmen's wedding, I had the unfortunate experience of losing my virginity to a teenage girl whose family sent her to work as a slave for our older neighbors. I say she was a slave because she wasn't paid anything, and although her hard labor was supposed to be compensated with free schooling, she never received that.

The unfortunate ugly reality is that slavery is still very much present in Bohio. In my opinion, there are more slaves now than during slavery times. By slaves, I mean children who are given up by their parents, poor people who live in the countryside or who do not have the best means, to other families who supposedly will provide a better life for their kids. In return for the child's labor, the family or individual is to provide the slave kids with an education. But ninety percent of the time, that never happens. Or if it does, the education provided is severely subpar to what the elite's kids receive. The slave kids go to school for only a couple hours a day, while the rich people's kids have school from seven a.m. to two o'clock in the afternoon, a full day. At the end of each day, three or four o'clock in the afternoon, the little slave kids who work so hard have to get themselves together and go to night school. The night school system is not as educative as the regular schools even in America, in Bohio, it's far worse.

At the time, the girl, who was six years older than me (about the same age as Flight 191), came home from school one day and decided to take a seven-year-old boy's virginity. She forced me to have sex with her when I was sent to keep her company while her slave holders were away.. Where we lived there were too many houses and not enough room to allow for healthy boundaries.

I didn't know any better so I went along with it, but after she had abused me, my penis was bleeding. I didn't know what the heck was going on. I had nobody to tell this to. I couldn't tell Flight 191 because she would likely tell Surrogate and I'd get my butt whipped. I could have possibly told Red

October but, again, I didn't want to get my butt whipped, because I'd obviously done something wrong although I didn't know what it was. So I kept it to myself, and the abuse continued; she did it many more times. Because I had nobody to talk to, I let it go until we moved away.

And then there was a girl who lived across the hallway from us in the world's smallest cul-de-sac. She was staying with her older brother, James, who was a schoolteacher, and his wife and young son. His wife was also a schoolteacher, but much duller than the average person. People called James "Maitre" (Professor in French) and he loved that title very much. Maitre James was very nosy, and often repeated unchecked rumors or hurtful gossip. He knew people spoke ill of him due to his babbling lips, but he didn't seem to care. Things were very mundane at this time and that must have been his way of bringing excitement into his boring home life.

His younger sister, who was sixteen, was staying with him at the time. She attempted to have sex with me soon after the abuse by the first girl had stopped. She grabbed my penis and wouldn't let go. She claimed to have had sex with Red October many times and proclaimed that he enjoyed it and so would I. She told me this while mounting me like a riding bull. I was half her age. I couldn't get an erection and that frustrated her; she acted like her life depended on this happening. I was scared and felt completely powerless.

Again I told no one. I felt unsafe in that house and didn't share my shameful secret with another living soul. I had no close friends, no mother or father to defend me. I was alone.

The situation of having no one to talk to is not foreign to me. I believe I shouldn't have been so used to it as a child, and, unfortunately, I am still way too familiar with it as we speak. I'm still struggling even now to create a proper support system. This situation really started when I was assaulted at seven years old and I had blood coming out of my penis and couldn't tell anyone. I was scared. I had nowhere to go; I had nobody to talk to.

- Moving Backwards -

We stayed for a little while at that house in Site Chovèl, and then we moved to Ruelles Capois, in Vertieres (vètyè). It was across from where the famous monuments of freedom are. This is where the last battle between Bohio and Napoleon's troops took place in 1803, when Napoleon's incumbents got their butts whipped by untrained former slaves who had a serious thirst for freedom and preferred death to slavery. Napoleon retreated all his troops from the Caribbean's richest country, and, within a few weeks of his defeat, he sold the Louisiana Territory to the newly formed United States of America for a measly fifteen million dollars. After beating Napoleon's forces, Bohio proclaimed its independence on January 1st of 1804. So that was a very monumental area (no pun intended).

We; Surrogate, Forgetful, Flight 191, Red October and I, lived there for a while — until the twins arrived in November of 1994.

Psychopath and Surrogate were really casual about the pregnancy: "Oh, okay, let's have another kid." My thought was, You aren't taking care of the four kids you have — why would you want to have another one? Of course, as soon as they intended to have another one, they got two more, and Challenged and Frivolous were born as the constellation of Scorpius was behind the Sun.

We were living on barely two hundred U.S. dollars a year, and now there were six kids, plus other people to feed. Financially, things got more complicated and much harder to bear. The twins made everything worse.

That was also around the time I realized that something might be going on with my brain that was different from other kids. Flight 191 was one of the first individuals to acknowledge my intellectual abilities, although without telling me so.

Flight 191, who was in high school, needed me to correct her papers and help her study. She'd give me the study guides for her midterms so I could sort of tutor her and help her get ready for the upcoming exams. She also enlisted my help with her homework assignments. I was constantly correcting her papers and even helping her study, whatever the subject was. I'd help her, but as for people helping me study, that never happened. I was always the one who helped my other siblings. Never did any family members help me with my homework or assignments.

Besides schoolwork, I also helped Flight 191 write personal correspondence. She wrote many letters to boyfriends, whoever she was dating at the time. I would edit her writing for better flow and clarity and give her constructive criticism.

Her longest, and by far most controversial, relationship was with a guy named Kenny. I thought he was the definition of fugly. He was very fugly with a smart tongue. He was a bad boy. My sister loved herself a bad boy. Surrogate hated him, and that only pushed my sister closer to him. They were together on and off for more than three years.

I got to know Kenny on an intimate level, way more than I wanted to. No preteens should ever be subjected to such mature language or situations. His letters to Flight 191 were often very sexually explicit and graphic in nature. I read through them for her and always came up with the perfect reply to his many requests for sexual favors or his odd declarations. I never told him that I was behind most of those raunchy replies, because I already felt awkward in his presence. I began to feel almost as if I was dating the guy. He cut my hair for me a few times; since he was dating my sister, that was customary, but I was uncomfortable around him.

One particular favorite pastime of Flight 191 was a game called "Jeu de correspondance" or JWET KORESPONDANS. It was THE game for hormonal and horny teenagers. It entailed an even number of young people of relationship age being paired up and writing back and forth to one another while never divulging their identities. At the end of the game a big party would take place and the organizers would reveal the names. The longest game I heard of took over two years before the reveal party happened. Often, the couples who had been corresponding stayed together after being in touch for so long and getting to know one another so intimately. Some participated mostly for the potential to hook up with someone new. I never played because I never believed in "buying a cat in a sack." Being dirt poor and too broke to afford the flower-scented stationery needed to sexually attract the so-called "classy" women also played a major role in keeping me out.

It was my job to read each of my sister's letters, however long, and then make my corrections and explain to her why those corrections needed to be made for the letter to flow better and for things to make more sense. I was not only expected to help Flight 191 with her papers, help her study and retain her information, but I also had to do my own schoolwork. Schools in Bohio are different from those in the U.S. During this time, in Bohio, memorization was key. There were no computers, no laptops, no phones, none of that. We literally had to memorize whatever it was we needed to learn. Even if it was five or six chapters of information that we needed to know by heart for the next week or whenever it was, we had to memorize it. I had to memorize my sister's information so I could give her constructive criticism about it, and I had to memorize mine at the same time. I thought every nine-year-old was doing this for his older sister. I didn't consider my ability to comprehend and interpret subjects that should have been far above me academically to be out of the norm.

* * *

I couldn't have any friends because Surrogate felt nobody was good enough. Though Surrogate was poor, she had a discriminatory policy of not allowing me to mingle with people she deemed inferior to us. She created a caste system all our own, a self-alienation. We were segregated from those who had slightly less economic potential, or who measured slightly lower on the socio-economic scale than we did. The goal was to always reach upward and try to interact with rich people — or people who obviously possessed more than us. More might have been fifty dollars. If they had fifty dollars more than us, we were supposed to engage with them because they could potentially help us out financially in the future.

I never agreed with that philosophy, and I constantly disobeyed her orders. At one point, I only hung out with the boys she forbade me to. This meant I got my butt whipped all the time, just for hanging out with those on the do-not-hang-out-with list. That list was extensive; the forbidden list included nearly all the boys from the entire neighborhood, while the list of people we should hang out with had a handful of names.

The irony was that ninety-nine percent of the people on the should-hang-out-with list were bullies. They would bully me and physically hit me, but I had no one to tell about the abuse. Surrogate would force me to go talk to them. And if I refused, I'd get my butt whipped. And by butt, I mean head, body, wherever; I'd get hit with whatever was nearby. I was being bullied by the people I was supposed to kiss up to, but the people I thought were cool and wanted to hang out with were not on the approved list.

Nothing bad ever happened between the forbidden boys and myself. They didn't act stuck up or look down their noses at me. I was treated fairly by them; therefore I chose to hang out with them despite the imminent threat to my life. It was liberating to me to fight off discrimination that was unfounded and wrong in my eyes. I felt they were being judged for things that were out of their control; their families' low financial standing shouldn't be the reason why they were assumed to be troublemakers.

I knew the beatings were coming and I accepted them with open arms because I believed in doing the right thing regardless of the negative consequences. I believed in this then and I still do today. Hanging out with those boys was the right thing to do. So, I did it.

And who was the main person telling Surrogate whenever I hung out with people who were on the do-not-hang-out-with list? Of course it was my wonderful sister, Forgetful. Forgetful never skipped a beat in her reporting to Surrogate. She was our family's very own version of Tekashi 6ix9ine. Not one of her siblings was safe; she snitched until she ran out of breath. On more than one occasion, she inadvertently snitched on herself.

She never let things go. She always snitched on everyone. She loved to snitch on us, embellish stories, or make up lies so we would get whipped. She would do her conferences with Surrogate and receive her rewards of candy or money and praises. I would see her eyes light up when she heard the first screams coming from the locked room when any of us was getting a senseless beating.

My earliest memory of her devilish ways dates back to when she was two and half years old, during the winter of 1990. Flight 191 and Red October were sitting at the small dining room table, drawing. Our main source of light while indoors was a kerosene-powered makeshift glass lamp. I vividly remember my two older siblings cautioning Forgetful about her movements near the table. They repeatedly told her to keep away from the opening on top of the lamp as the consequences would be dire. She tried over and over to defy them and get herself injured. After many failed attempts, she succeeded in hurting herself. The flames caught the side of her head and burned some of her hair. Her edges never grew back. The stench overpowered my sense of smell for several minutes. She cried and we all tried to calm her down. She stopped crying. As soon as Surrogate walked through the door, she started crying harder than when the incident first occurred. Fake tears and sobs. She managed to get a few words out, while vigorously pointing at Flight 191 and Red October as the perpetrators. I didn't get whipped that time. However, the winter of 1990 was the beginning of Forgetful's dictator-like reign over all of us. From that point forward, her status as the favorite was cemented into our brains and she never let us forget it. We were older than her, but we feared her slithering tongue.

About six months after the above incident, she began picking up many bad habits, one after another, at our butts' expense. One in particular stood out. After the food was accordingly rationed, she would only chew the meat given to her, but not swallow it. She swallowed only the resulting juice then spit out the rest. Then she would demand a piece, if not all, of the meat that any of us had left so she could do the same with it. At that time, we were financially forced to be vegetarians during most of the week. Meat was hard to come by, therefore, we were always reluctant to give up our small morsels of chicken, beef or goat meat. She always won these battles because our refusal often triggered an impromptu beating by Surrogate. If these incidents occurred in Surrogate's absence, Forgetful would report our "disrespect" upon her return and the beating of all culprits took place soon after. The "disrespect," in Forgetful's eyes, was disobeying her orders; she would recount the story with the facts twisted, and her fake cries always present when she went to snitch on us. Within the household, Forgetful was part of the Bourgeoisie and we, the Proletariat.

The main mode of transportation in Bohio was via tap-tap or kamyonèt. A kamyonèt is a compact pickup truck that has been converted into a passenger carrying vehicle with a roof and sometimes a sound system. They are always painted with colorful designs and important life or spiritual messages. They are beautifully-painted from roof to mug flaps or wheels. It felt as if there was an unofficial competition to see who could create the brightest or most colorful tap-tap. Forgetful was sneaky and stingy. Whenever she'd travel by tap-tap, she would try to trick good Samaritans into paying her fare. She always hid her money deep inside her oversized book bag and would make a show of searching around in it for her fare. Seeing her struggling to get her fare, more often than not, kind strangers would offer to pay for her. She only paid the fare a few times a month. She would brag about how she conned the passengers as usual and count her unspent money as a victory in her war against humanity.

Soccer was and remains the national sport in Bohio. Surrogate forbade me to play. She must have instructed Forgetful to spy on me and report back to her. Somehow, Forgetful always knew when I played, even when she wasn't within sight. At times, I went to play miles away from the house to prevent her from seeing me. Somehow she always did, and reported to Surrogate. The senseless beating would commence within minutes of her arrival home from work. The dagger was when Forgetful reported my activities for the day when they involved playing soccer with the boys from the do-not-play-with list; then the hatred in Surrogate's eyes burned brighter than ever and the beatings took a different form, escalating from a regular beating to slave-breaking. The only boys that weren't on that list were my bullies.

In 2001, when Forgetful was fifteen years old, her boyfriend, Jude Bernard, threatened to put a bullet in my head. He told me, "I'm tired of you interfering with my love life. I can't hang out with my girlfriend because she keeps leaving my side every time you appear." He continued, "If it wasn't for the fear of eternal damnation, I would take my father's gun and blow your brains out. Trust me, that's how tired of you I am."

Immediately after he made this declaration, I ran and told Surrogate of my impending demise. She did nothing. She told Forgetful to talk to him and ask him not to kill me. That's it.

I wasn't allowed to have a girlfriend, but not only did Forgetful have a boyfriend that everyone knew of, Jude's father was a big fat jerk who constantly looked down his nose at people. His mother was pretentious and was up on her high horse every day. I didn't understand why Forgetful could date but I couldn't. It recently hit me: the Bernards were better off than we were. The father worked for some gas station as a General Manager and he had a company-provided, brand new motorcycle to transport him to and from work. Had I dated someone who was financially better off than we were, then it would have been ok in Surrogate's point of view. I never did such a thing; I wasn't an opportunist back then and I'm not one now.

Jude wasn't only a homicidal, effeminate, pretentious jerk, he was also a liar. That same summer in 2001, a group of boys and I climbed into a tap-tap, headed to Odikap. I knew some of them from the neighborhood. The driver decided to go wash the vehicle at the shallow end of the river where the poor orphans were ever present to wash cars for a few bucks — enough to get some food to quiet down the loud rumbling in their intestines.

One of these boys taught me how to swim in the dirty stream behind our house. The stream was directly between the River of Odikap and the Caribbean Sea on the other side. He asked me to help him finish washing the car so we could all get back home faster. I did. I didn't ask to get paid for helping since he was my friend and I barely did anything. The driver dropped us off back where he picked us up and that was it. Or so I thought. The feminine, hip-heaving bastard told his loose-lipped girlfriend of my presence at the river. Between the two of them they concluded that I went to the river to wash cars for money. The fabricated story made its way to Surrogate's ears. Without probable cause, cross examination or any real proof, within seconds of hearing this lie, Surrogate unleashed on me. She went crazy; she lost her mind. I couldn't understand a word she was saying, but the blood gushing out of my wounds was visibly real and the pain was unbearable. She even bit me on the arm like a wild dog on a mission to feed its family.

She never told me what this specific beating was all about until days later. And then it hit me: that soon-to-be-gay butthole was at the river that day. I wondered, if he had seen the whole interaction, why would he lie like this? I remembered him threatening my life less than two months earlier; this must have been his way of getting revenge on me for interfering with his love life. Since he decided to not kill me, he enlisted Surrogate's help via Forgetful's slippery tongue to get the job done. His mission proceeded without any difficulty because it took nothing at all to get me beaten down to a bloody pulp. Everyone in the neighborhood knew about Surrogate's abhorrence towards me. They tested and confirmed this fact many times.

Jean and Jules are Psychopath's younger brothers. During the winter break in 2001, they came back home for a short while. Two hours after I left my house to go to theirs in Monben Latay, a neighborhood clown by the name of T-Ken saw Surrogate walking by his house. He stopped her to tell her that I was recently there causing a raucous, less than five minutes earlier. The fact was; I had never caused any trouble there, and I was miles away, per Surrogate's request. This was the only time that someone's lies didn't get me

VERLY E. DOLCE

whipped for hours. Surrogate told me the story the next day when I came back. I wasn't surprised by these crazy accusations; I was relieved that she refrained from beating me senselessly for once. I hoped that day, at least, she could see right through the lies and see that I was a good kid. She never apologized for the hundreds of times she believed everyone else over me, or acted without asking me what happened first.

Two days later, I overheard her recounting the scenario to Flight 191 and she sounded a bit remorseful. Not enough to stop the beatings, but enough for her to say, "Can you believe this? That boy blatantly lied to get me to beat SonSonn for no reason

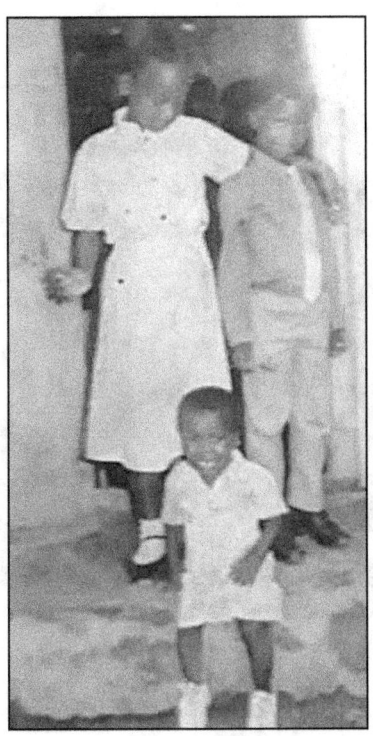

*In front of Grandma Rose's house in Laplange.
L to R, Flight 191, Red October right and me in front.
I was crying because they took the piece of Pain Gouden
from me to take the picture. Summer 1987*

*L to R, Frivolous, Challenged
and me in the middle, November 2001*

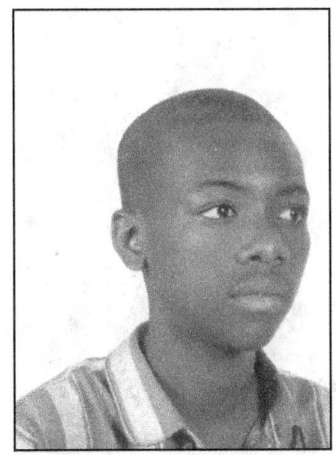

Sent to INS (Now, USCIS) January, 2002

*Two friends from Lycée Nationale Philippe Guerrier,
my High School in Bohio.
Patrick, Roger, and me in the middle.
March, 2002*

Psychopath right, next to my 13-year-old cousin Val, shortly after Brazil won the World Cup. July, 2002

In the parking lot of the brand-new Walmart where Psychopath worked in Norwalk. Pretending to drive the Green Plymouth Grand Voyager. Summer, 2003

Psychopath eating ice cream while holding on to the Plymouth Grand Voyager. Summer, 2003

Ms. Greene, Room 202, homeroom teacher for my senior year at Bassick. Fall, 2003-2004

Mr. Solis (ESL teacher) and Ngoc Nguyen, a Vietnamese friend.

After Graduating, Behind the Klein. Photo by Forgetful's social worker, Yvette. June 2004.

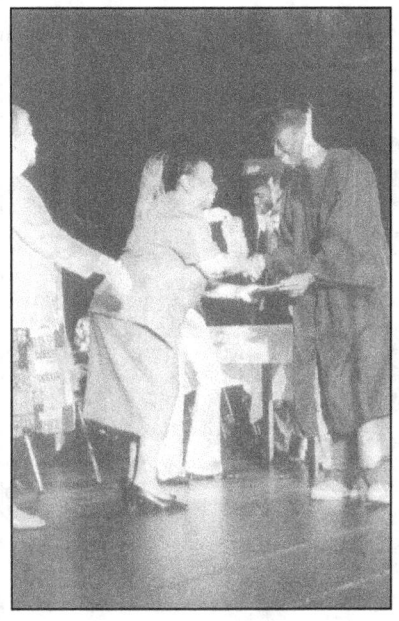

The Klein Memorial Auditorium. Receiving my diploma from Bassick High School. June, 2004

On Scofield Ave. Next to the Haitian Church. Summer, 2005

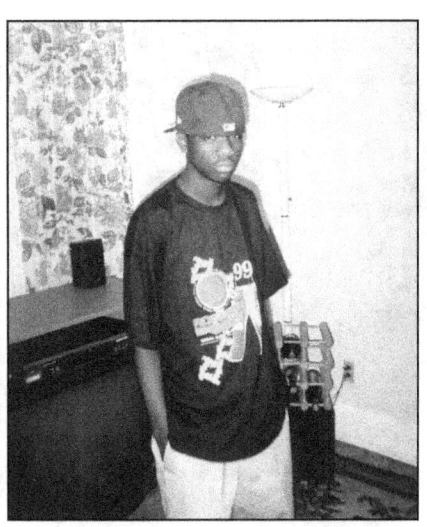

Taken by Nigel at 1491 Pembroke St. after graduating high school. Summer, 2004

*On Scofield Ave. Next to the Haitian Church.
Summer, 2005*

*Verly and Granma Rose
Kanpela Studio, Haiti, April 1, 2009*

Granma April 1, 2009

Uncle Sam, Granma Rose and I. April 1, 2009

First Month of dating Goldie. May 2009

One-year anniversary with Goldie. Summer, 2010

Family picture session for Goldie's birthday. Ventura, CA., 2017

US Navy Boot Camp Graduation. Illinois. Verly and Surrogate. November, 2012

Conejo Creek North Park, Thousand Oaks CA. January 5, 2020.
Photo credit: Samer Yousef Photography.

Ventura College Graduation, Summit Park, Santa Clarita CA. May 20, 2019
Photo credit: Samer Yousef Photography.

- Babylon -

After the coup d'état of 1991, economic sanctions were placed on the country and U.S. Marines descended on Bohio. They began busily taking over everything, including the women, many of whom later gave birth to half-white babies whose fathers they'd never see again. Restrictions were placed on the amount of money that could be sent from Babylon to Bohio. Two hundred dollars was the maximum allowed. When a unilateral military occupation takes place and another country sends soldiers to take over an entire government, they can do stuff like that. The U.S. government did that.

The only way to send more than $200 from Babylon to Bohio was to send it under somebody else's name. You could do this under two or three different names; that way it wouldn't trigger a red flag and you wouldn't get denied.

One of the money transfers was issued in my name, and I used my school ID to go pick it up with Surrogate. I was confused about why it was done this way. It was explained to me that there was an embargo, or political sanctions (or whatever they called it at the time) and because of political unrest, Marines had landed and were basically controlling the entire country.

Around that same time, I started to develop my patriotic interests and decided if I ever went to Babylon I would join the armed forces. I had met one of the occupying Marines who was from Bohio; he spoke the language. It was mind boggling to me that he was part of the Marines. I had never really envisioned going to Babylon; I never expected to meet someone who was from there and who spoke my language. I was intrigued and I spoke to him for quite a while. He said something very meaningful to me: "If you ever make it to Babylon and you have the right papers, odds are you have a very, very good chance of joining the armed forces. They want and need people like you." I took his words to heart.

Psychopath typically had many women in the same city at the same time. Shells was a devoted side chick; she stuck around even though she was aware of his marriage to the Cougar and knew that they had a kid and shared a bed. Shells didn't care about that; in fact, whenever he didn't spend the night at the Cougar's house, Shells had the audacity to call and taunt her, bragging that her husband was in Shells' bed and there was nothing she could do about it.

After our many abandonments by Psychopath, big-booty Shells finally talked him into helping us get to Babylon. Shells often bragged about how she got him to go through proper immigration channels and file the paperwork to get us there. Regrettably, only Forgetful and I came.

We landed at JFK international airport on November 26, 2002, shortly after 7:00 p.m. I followed the other passengers to Customs. I knew not one word of English, but I tried to act like I knew what I was doing. Forgetful was gazing up at the ceiling as if awestruck. I grabbed her hand and told her to act like she belonged because this was our new place. For me, it had to work. I couldn't go back home. There would be no warm embrace from a loving mother waiting for me if things didn't work out.

After clearing Customs and experiencing our first-ever escalator ride, we arrived at the carousel to await our luggage, which was one shared suitcase. The brown nineteen seventies-style leather luggage was light as a feather; even in my malnourished state, I easily carried it with one hand. Most of the contents were hers. I had brought only a few t-shirts, a couple of collared shirts and one pair of jeans.

The 60-mile journey from the airport to Bridgeport is typically a 75-minute car ride, but our trip took almost four hours longer. It felt like we were running a marathon.

Psychopath was supposed to meet our plane, but as he was leaving Shells' house at 2:00 a.m. that morning, he was t-boned by a drunk driver. He had only the state-mandated minimal or basic liability insurance so he didn't qualify for a loaner car from the insurance company, and of course he couldn't afford a rental car. He called to inform us of the accident, but simply said he was out of the hospital and was still coming to pick us up. He failed to mention where he was coming from and that the arrangements for transportation had been drastically changed.

The waiting wouldn't have been so bad if we were properly dressed for the frigid weather of New England. I wore black slacks and dress shoes with thin socks, and a black t-shirt under a navy-blue blazer that was two sizes too big for me. When Psychopath finally arrived at the airport, he handed us some old direct-from-the-unwanted-clothes-pile jackets for us to put on. The Cougar later informed me that the clothing he brought for us was what he used to cover his car windows with to prevent ice accumulation during the rough winter months. That's how little he thought of us.

He led us to a tram, which took us to a bus that delivered us to a shorter train that led us to a subway train, which got us to Grand Central Station in the middle of Manhattan. From there we took the Metro North train to Stamford, Connecticut. The train dropped us off; we waited at least another forty-five minutes for another train coming from Danbury that would take us to the old bus/train station in downtown Bridgeport. Once there, we took a yellow cab, and finally arrived in Bridgeport after one o'clock in the morning.

Psychopath and Cougar lived at 760 Atlantic Street, Apartment 10-D in Bridgeport, Connecticut, with their kid, Spoiled, who was the first of our family to be born in Babylon. The four-story building was painted all white, inside and out. We lived on the second floor with a sad back view of the center court and parking spaces.

Two days later, on November 28, 2002, it was Thanksgiving. Via the number six bus, Psychopath brought Forgetful and me to the United Congregational Church of Bridgeport at the corner of Park Avenue and State Street for a free warm meal and to pick up some overused, unwanted clothes that the church folks often gave away to commoners, miscreants and the homeless population. They welcomed us, speaking in very soft tones so as to not set off our crazy or something. I later discovered that these unusually nice white people were as rare in Bridgeport as finding a unicorn at the end of a sparkling rainbow in the middle of Detroit, Michigan.

We sat down, and they seemed happy to feed us. It could have been that they were being condescending or acting like they were superior to us; I was too hungry to care or try to figure out which it was. Our plates were overfilled with food I'd never heard of before. Cranberry sauce, stuffing, yams, mashed potatoes, and so on. Lots of food foreign to us. We ate it all. Within one hour of arriving, Forgetful fell very ill and the churchgoers called an ambulance to take her to Bridgeport Hospital because she didn't look so good.

For over three hours, I sat in the emergency waiting room of Bridgeport Hospital, all alone. Psychopath had taken the opportunity to check himself in as well in order to get an IV drip because he was feeling a little tired. He had health insurance at the time, Blue Cross-Blue Shield of Connecticut, through his job at a discount department store. I didn't know any English; I couldn't speak to anyone; I simply smiled and nodded like an idiot to everything they said to me. I wondered the entire time, What in the heck is going on back there? He came out looking refreshed and ready to take on the world.

When we left, we took two more buses to make our way to Shells' house. Shells had three kids, two boys and a girl, but it seemed her proudest and most important role was being Psychopath's mistress. She asked us questions, we met her kids, and then took two more buses back to the 575-sq. ft., one-bedroom apartment the five of us now shared.

The culture shock was instantaneous, but we managed. By December 2, 2002, we were enrolled at Bassick High School to continue our schooling and help us learn the language and culture. We had the pleasure of enjoying the luxurious public transportation system that the wonderful city of Bridgeport had to offer during the coldest days of my life. I had to adjust by dressing in multiple layers because freezing my nipples off didn't sound like an ideal way to die.

About a week before I flew from Bohio to Babylon, Surrogate had sat me down and, in front of everyone, told me, "You will never amount to anything. You will become a drug dealer as soon as you get to the next country. You're gonna get arrested and you're gonna get put in prison and within a year you'll be deported back. And once you get deported, I will not support you. I will abandon you like I've always wanted to." And she continued, "I am not hopeful; I am not happy about you leaving. I don't have any faith in you; I don't believe that you're gonna ever help me when you get to wherever you're going, since you're just going to start selling drugs and get arrested. The only thing I'm happy about is that you are gonna be gone and I will no longer have to feed you and give you clothes and take care of you. For that one-year time that you'll be gone, it'll be a sigh of relief for me to no longer take care of this worthless piece of shit of a son that I never wanted, I adopted that's not even my own, that I've been trying to put in an orphanage for so long."

Real words said from a mother to her son, her first kid, her only son. Real words. A real declaration. Not making it up. I did have to translate it, but this was her real declaration. Those were some hurtful words to hear from your supposed mother, even a surrogate; no one should be saying that to a seventeen-year-old, especially one who had no record, no criminal record, never drank, never smoked, never sold drugs, never did any drugs. It was extremely uncalled for; there was no reason for it. But those were the statements made by Surrogate to me.

Red October pulled me aside after she was done bashing me and said, "You need to prove her wrong. I know you will, and once you do, you need to forgive her, and do the opposite of what she says. Send her money and make her bite her tongue. That will make her cry and realize she's a terrible person, and she'll tell you how wrong she was and how sorry she is." Then, he hugged me. I needed that hug.

I'm still waiting for that apology from Surrogate. I'm not going to hold my breath because I will pass out and die before that day comes.

Now that she also lives here in Babylon, she maintains an obviously-fake act of being a supportive mother. In 2016, I went to visit her in Norwalk, Connecticut and she tenderly touched my face and hair for the first time in my life. It was the weirdest touch I've ever received. I felt like screaming. I felt like I was a kid about to be kidnapped by a stranger and this strange lady was touching me in a way my actual mother should have way back when. Surrogate never touched me tenderly. She never held me — unless you count the way she would grab me and hold on at the beginning of her senseless beatings when she went crazy like a madwoman.

I played along with her caring mother act for as long as I could, requiring twelve to fifteen beers or two full bottles of red wine to stomach her fakeness.

The reason I tell this story about Surrogate is because although the same exact words were not necessarily uttered by my future wife, Goldie, she depicted the exact same mentality and behavior towards me, but added to it. Goldie was Surrogate, a bit younger; however, more bitter, slightly better educated, but not by much. The only way I could find another woman more like Surrogate would be to clone Surrogate.

Shortly after I arrived in Babylon, I attempted to, and eventually did, join the U.S. Navy, and was able to serve my new country with pride.

While attending Bassick High School, during the Spring of 2004 career fair, a lot of military branches showed up while not many great employers came. The recruiters from all of the branches were present except for the Air Force. Out of all of them, the recruiter from the Navy was the nicest, a well-spoken Hispanic man named Rodney. He asked us to call him by his first name, and to this day I do not know his last name. I thought the Navy was the best branch because of how nice the entire recruiting office staff was to me when I went to visit the so-called career center. It was on Main Street, across from the food-poisoning-center known as Red Lobster.

I took the practice test in the office more than five times, each time scoring a little better than the last. But since I was new to the country and culture, I could barely score high enough to warrant a trip to the Springfield Military Entrance Processing Station (MEPS) in Chicopee, Massachusetts.

The Navy recruiters never gave up on me. They encouraged me to study harder and told me to make sure I graduated high school on time so they could ship me out to go live out my dream of being a sailor in the United

States Navy. I went to the main branch of the Bridgeport Public Library and checked out the latest ASVAB (Armed Services Vocational Aptitude Battery) prep book. Over several months, I renewed it often and made it a point to study and retain the information therein.

I ended up not joining the Navy after high school like I'd intended, and instead went to work at Radio Shack in Fairfield. I tried attending school at Housatonic Community College while working, but finding it impossible to do both, I dropped out of school and focused on working — more than one job at once — so I could lead a mediocre life below the poverty line. This was my situation for nearly a decade of living in Bridgeport. I moved to nearly all the neighborhoods of the Park City except for the North end; I was always too broke to afford a place there; even a frigid, illegally-rented basement was out of my financial reach.

During Spring of 2009, I enrolled in Culinary School at Lincoln Technical Institute in Shelton. I graduated the following year with Honors. It was a two-year program condensed into an 18-months jammed-packed schedule. Right after graduating, my job prospects were still not up to par. To further my education, I scheduled a meeting with Dr. Failla, the then Director of the Hospitality Management program at Norwalk Community College, in October 2010. Dr. Failla made me the following promise: "We're gonna help you become a gentleman and a scholar." I enrolled in full time classes at NCC beginning in the Spring 2011 semester. Dr. Failla helped me to transfer as many credits from Lincoln Tech as possible. I didn't have to take any of the cooking classes due to my recent graduation from a well-respected, local culinary arts program. I needed to finish all the core, college-level classes to get my Associate's Degree in Restaurant and Foodservice Management. I buckled down, studied hard, stayed focused, and I was able to walk during graduation with colleagues that had been in the Hospitality program long before I arrived. In about three years, I completed two degrees, Culinary Arts at Lincoln Tech and Hospitality Management at Norwalk Community College. I was ecstatic about my latest accomplishments, but not so much about my future.

I was still working odd jobs without a clear path to the bright future I had envisioned for myself. I never stopped thinking about what my life could have been like had I enlisted.

As luck or fate would have it, one January morning in 2012, within the walls of Norwalk Community College, near the student-run dining room, I bumped into Soto, who had been an E-5 recruiter along with Rodney back in the day. Soto had made Chief (E-7) and returned to run the recruiting office some eight years later. Somehow, he remembered me from all those years ago. He called me by my last name, "Dolce, right?" I said, "Aren't you Soto?" We talked for a brief period and he asked if I was still interested in joining the Navy. My heart in my throat, I said, "Yes!" and he gave me his business card and invited me back to the now reconfigured office with brand new furniture and staff. I was in my last semester at NCC so it made perfect sense to revisit the opportunity I had thought was lost for all of eternity.

One week later, I walked back into the same office that had almost been responsible for changing my life forever. Soto introduced me to a rather short female recruiter from one of the Caribbean islands. Since Soto was the BOSS now, he had become a pencil pusher. I took the practice test and scored a 69 out of 99, more than twice as high as the last time I had taken it many moons before. We made plans for the recruiter to drop me off at the Springfield MEPS on Monday, February 13th to be processed on the 14th, Valentine's Day. Everything proceeded without any complications, and by the end of the day I had finally achieved my longest life goal, something I'd wanted ever since I met the Marine in 1994. I was on track to become a sailor in the U.S. Navy. I was part of the coveted Delayed Entry Program (DEP).

I had dreamt of this moment for years, and for this reason, when I arrived at boot camp on August 30th of 2012, I was in awe and shock. For more than three days I felt like I was having an out-of-body experience. I couldn't believe what was happening to me and my brain refused to accept the fact that I had achieved the greatest accomplishment in the world. I'm a U.S. Navy Sailor. ME, a kid from the slums of Haiti, who struggled tremendously in the streets of Bridgeport, Connecticut and lived below the poverty line most of my life, I am SAILOR! In the GREATEST Navy in the world.

Achieving this longtime goal meant so much to me, it is one reason why it's hard for me to talk to anyone who does not understand my sacrifice or where I came from to be where I am today. Some people belittle everything I went through because, to them, it was nothing. My joining the Navy wasn't by accident; it happened because I worked really, really, really hard and I did exactly what the Marine had told me to do. I always remembered him encouraging me, "You should do it, man. You're gonna do great." I kept my nose clean and I stayed on course, and I stayed on target. I was determined to do this.

I am doing great. I love it and I'm doing it. I'm proud of accomplishing this longtime goal, and I don't have patience for anyone who doesn't agree with my joining the Navy or doing anything to better myself. I felt the patriotism and willingness to do my part to help my new country.

We need people to volunteer; otherwise your overprivileged butt will be drafted and sent to countries you don't want to go to. So be thankful, be grateful to those who are making the sacrifice so you can sit at your wonderful home in the safety of your parents' proverbial womb or wherever you sit now. Don't criticize those of us who have literally made the ultimate sacrifice, and those of us who literally sacrifice ourselves for your freedom. This, our freedom is not free. Somebody has to pay for it. Nothing in life is free. You may not have to pay for it yourself, you may get a discount, you may get a very low interest rate on it, it could be well priced, but it is not free. Nothing is free.

VERLY E. DOLCE

- No More Mister Nice Guy -

My entire life, I've been dealing with ungrateful people. I'm still struggling to grasp the true meaning behind their ways. Maybe I'm still too naïve; maybe I'm still not mature enough. I don't know what the reason is, but I still do not understand these people.

In 2004, shortly before I graduated high school, a Canadian punk rock band released an album titled Still Not Getting Any. The musicians were in Canada; I was living in Bridgeport, Connecticut, and they were living my life. The featured single was called "Welcome to My Life." The lead singer sang about how he was feeling down and was being kicked while he was down. I felt I'd never heard anything so true. Never have any other song lyrics resonated with me so completely.

Some of the lyrics:

Do you ever feel like breaking down?
Do you ever feel out of place?
Like somehow you just don't belong
And no one understands you.
No, you don't know what it's like
When nothing feels alright
You don't know what it's like to be like me
To be hurt, to feel lost
To be left out in the dark
To be kicked when you're down
To feel like you've been pushed around
To be on the edge of breaking down
And no one there to save you
No you don't know what it's like

Welcome to my life.

Essentially, these lyrics described my life. It was true then; it's been true my entire life, and it's still true today. Still, no one seems to understand me, though I have made an above and beyond effort to understand other people, put their needs first, to the point where I have neglected myself. I've always put everyone else's emotions, feelings, concerns and problems way ahead of mine. It's been less than a year since I started toying with the idea of taking care of myself so that I can better help others, because putting myself first is still a foreign concept for me.

I was seventeen when I got my first job in April of 2003. I'd been in the country for barely five months and spoke little English, but I had to somehow come up with enough money to support myself. Psychopath and Shells both worked at the new Walmart in Norwalk. They'd been hired together in 2003, pre-grand opening of the store. Walmart was down the street from Burger King, which was next to an old Army and Navy surplus store, which was across the street from an Old Navy store. I don't know where I got the courage or even the intelligence to do this, but I applied for a job at Burger King. After filling out an application, I asked to speak to the hiring manager. When the manager came out, I looked him in the eye while I shook his hand, and proceeded to tell him about myself. His name was Mike.

Mike asked me two very simple questions: "Are you in high school?"

"Yes."

"Can you start on Thursday?"

"Yes."

He then said, "You're hired. Come on Thursday. Bring a pair of black pants. Bring your Social Security card and your work authorization" (i.e., green card or other paperwork showing that I was legally allowed to work in the country).

It was the briefest job interview I've ever had, lasting no more than two minutes. Obviously Mike saw something in me and he hired me. I was a cashier at that Burger King for some time.

Getting to work was really hard, especially on the days I wasn't in school, because our house on Pembroke was inconvenient for public transportation. I had to take three buses to get there and three more to get back home. Fortunately, Mike understood, and I felt it was a really good situation for me, although not in terms of pay because I was making only $6.90 an hour, and because I was still in high school, I couldn't work more than 20 hours per week. The most I ever made in any week was $180 once. I had worked my butt off that week and, needless to say, my wonderful father took most of it and I never saw that money. Fleet Bank (later acquired by Bank of America) was his bank and the bank used by my Burger King franchisee at the time. Psychopath always took me to the bank to cash my paychecks. He did this to make sure he took all my hard-earned dollars. Regardless of how much money I made, he kept most of it. The most money he ever let me keep was $40.

I was generous with whatever money I had left, often giving some to other high school kids. I did this even though most of them lived at home and didn't have to work like I did, and I knew they only wanted the money so they could skip lunch and go buy junk food. The vending machines were filled with popular snacks and drinks like crackers, sunflower seeds in the shell that created a big mess and Fruitopia (a fruit punch flavored drink). While I was making all these generous transactions, people probably assumed I had money — I didn't. I never had enough left to buy these snacks for myself. I had barely enough to survive on and I had to save the little I had left so I could pay the rent and the bills. I guess it's odd, now that I'm thinking about it, that I never enjoyed the fruits of my own labor.

I was mainly eating Chef Boyardee canned ravioli, canned Spaghetti-O's, and canned pasta and meatballs in tomato sauce, and packets of ramen noodles. I bought the food at Price Rite, which wasn't too expensive. The ravioli cost 79 cents a can and the ramen noodles were eight for a dollar so I could afford two for lunch. For dinner I'd scoop two cans of ravioli onto a plate, heat it up and eat it. I spent around 25 cents for lunch (two ramen noodle packets, twelve and a half cents each) and $1.78 for dinner. If money was really low, I would have one can of ravioli for dinner. If I needed a late-night snack, or had to eat something in the early morning because the hunger was severe, I'd thaw one of the frozen taquitos that I kept around. They were kind of like soft tacos that Price Rite sold in big packs. They tasted like crap, but you could buy 50 of them for five dollars, a lot of food for little money. Needless to say, the quality was exactly what you paid for.

That was my diet, but throughout this whole process, I continued to give away money to people who obviously had more than I did.

We lived on Atlantic Street for less than six months. The fights between Psychopath and his Cougar wife were escalating and getting out of hand. During one of their physical altercations, I attempted to stop him from bashing her head in with a clothes iron and I got struck in the chest with the hot appliance.

Psychopath is no taller than five feet, five inches; he is a little fella with a very short fuse. The acts and crimes committed by that small-statured man are unforgivable and heinous to say the least. He is an ill-tempered nutjob who is unable to see the sheer amount of destruction he causes.

Forgetful wasn't completely innocent either, often fighting with the Cougar, forcing Psychopath to intervene. His solution was to move the two of us out, and often we were three because Spoiled lived with us fifty percent of the time.

Before the summer of 2003, the five of us had vacated the one-bedroom apartment that we'd been packed into like sardines. The Cougar moved in with her daughter, Spoiled, to a somehow tinier sixth-floor apartment at the Fairfield Gardens complex. The complex was on the block next to Bassick High School. Psychopath, Forgetful and I moved to 1489 Pembroke Street, next door to Shells' second-floor apartment at 1513 Pembroke. Cougar and Psychopath shared custody of Spoiled. I felt he mostly wanted her around to rightfully claim the Child Tax Credit from the Internal Revenue Service when he filed his taxes. The Cougar was tired of Spoiled's antics and shenanigans, she couldn't care less about her. This was obvious, and Psychopath used that to his advantage every chance he got. Our apartment was oddly configured: four independent rooms that had been converted to a rooming house. We had the first two rooms closest to the street, the only rooms that shared an internal door. We had roommates who shared the small kitchen and restroom with us. The landlord was a tall Haitian guy named Philip. The kitchen had a stench of despair and sadness loomed over the narrow hallway that connected the rooms to the half-and-half bath situation. The sink and toilet were placed together while the shower stood alone, across from Lolita's room.

Within six months of that move, the situation became unbearable for all involved. Psychopath's abuses escalated. Spoiled and Forgetful acted more and more entitled. Spoiled stopped going to middle school altogether. They both started smoking cigarettes; I caught them doing it. Forgetful and Spoiled started to regularly leave the house to go hang out with much older boys, and the list goes on.

Not long before Thanksgiving of 2003, Forgetful and Spoiled got into a heated altercation over Forgetful's brand new white Nike Air Force 1 High Top sneakers. They were returned by Spoiled uncleaned after a full day of walking in rainy weather. Spoiled was very ghetto, ratchet and privileged all at the same. A weird combination for someone who chose not to brush her teeth or shower for days. Their fight over boundaries became physical, and Forgetful's selfishness really emerged during the fight. She cussed out everybody, including Psychopath, who didn't take it too well. He punched her in the eye and she stormed out of the house. This happened around nine p.m. I saw her the next day at Bassick around ten a.m., but shortly after, she was removed from school for months. Due to the domestic abuse and the other heinous abuses committed by Psychopath, she was removed from the house by the Department of Children and Family. She was now a ward of the State of Connecticut and her stays at many foster homes soon followed. She came back to school only briefly, but we somehow graduated high school together in 2004. The whole thing was odd to me. I guess when you have the whole state on your side, what's a couple of skipped grades between friends? Her entire four-year private school college experience was paid for by the State, she told me. Her first apartment was furnished by them as well using government-backed all-inclusive vouchers at Bob's discount furniture.

I was succeeding academically, even though I was barely able to make it to class; and when I did, I was really tired because I had to work so many long hours. Most of the seniors didn't go to school past 11 a.m. or twelve noon, but I stayed until 2:30 p.m. Then I'd go to work, come home, and go right back to school in the morning.

Yes, I had to fake a few parental signatures to ask for some excused absences because my father wasn't in the house anymore and the school officials didn't know that. This started during the Fall of 2003, the beginning of my senior year. I found it to be a bit too easy to write the notes pretending to be this loser; the school administrators ate it all up. I was shocked and relieved at the same time.

I turned eighteen. The Department of Children and Family (DCF) of Fairfield County, Connecticut came and took both my sisters and, just like that, I was all by myself. In a big and foreign land.

Ivette, the DCF caseworker, asked my age when they came back with the police dogs to arrest Psychopath later that night. I told her I had turned 18 years old. Without skipping a beat, she said, "In that case, good luck to you!" I didn't believe she meant it because she said it with a smug face. She had the look of a bloodhound on a mission. She was a short, small-framed Haitian lady with a fake ponytail, disproportionately long, and an accent that she tried really hard to not let come out. I heard it. The four police officers with her seemed bothered and disappointed that they didn't find Psychopath. The neighbors had told me they were looking for him earlier. I had been at the library and didn't come home until the sun went down. They said the police had waited outside for a long time, hoping to catch him so they could take him away in handcuffs to the county jail on Madison Avenue.

He was gone; he'd suspected the raid would happen. Earlier that day, he'd threatened to kill the DCF case worker after she caught him unlawfully visiting Spoiled. How dumb is this guy? He threatened physical harm to a county government employee for doing her job.

He fled to New York City with only the clothes on his back and the olive-green late model Plymouth Grand Voyager minivan he'd bought eight months earlier. He was making weekly payments on it. I kept the book for these payments, $52 a week. I kept a record of when each payment was mailed to the vehicle title holder.

After Psychopath made a big mess of things, he escaped and ran off to Bohio to hide from the authorities, leaving fifty bucks in my bank account. The bank had a requirement that if your balance dropped below $200, you'd be charged a monthly fee. Psychopath took the money without telling me, and took the bank book with him also. It had taken many months for me to amass the $200 in the account; he took 75% of it after he forced his way into becoming an authorized user on my account.

This is an example of what I mean by being ungrateful and me still not understanding the world; even then, I still put others first. Even Psychopath, who I still sent money to regardless of the heinous acts I knew for sure he'd committed — and I also knew that he knew, I knew. Whenever possible, I also constantly sent money to Surrogate despite the way she treated me.

Soon after that debacle, the two rooms were split once more and now we had a four-room house being shared by five people. There were only those rooms and the tiny kitchen. Once the dust settled, on December 1, 2003, I heard a loud knock on the door; it was Philip, the landlord, who'd come to collect the rent. I didn't have it. I didn't know where my father was, and I was an unemployed high school senior with no job prospects or any money to my name. Philip told me the rooms would be divided and he'd let me keep the smaller room, but I had to start paying rent as soon as I received my first check. All utilities were included for $250 per month.

Philip came back later that day with materials needed to completely shut off the adjoining door. Lolita lived at the end of the hall with her husband, who was missing his right leg below the knee. His name was Ramon.

Next was Marlon's room, then Lolita's son-turned-daughter and I shared a wall. She moved into the bigger of the two rooms I had previously shared with my family. I couldn't afford the higher rent so I was confined to the six by ten-foot room in front of the street.

Lolita was a Dominican Republic citizen who went to Puerto Rico in search of American citizenship; Sophia was born there. Sophia told me stories of her first few sexual encounters with much older men on a park bench in Puerto Rico. One particular guy (her most loyal sex buddy) used to buy her the drugs to turn her into the woman she was when I met her. She said it had all started when she was only twelve years old. At the time of our talks, she was in her mid-twenties and had a completely female-looking body. Lolita met her husband there. She came to the U.S. as a citizen, since Puerto Ricans are legal U.S. citizens, as long as they have proper documentation.

Marlon was a divorced man who'd been kicked out of the home and was paying child support for his son. He was an avid smoker, but was a nice guy to me. His nickname for me was Baby Boy. The movie of the same title with Taraji P. Henson, Snoop Doggy Dogg and Tyrese Gibson had come out around the time we shared the house. He drank, and I believe he used to smoke a little reefer, nothing wrong with that, and once or twice a week the entire kitchen would be turned into a makeshift strip club where random strangers, most of them grown men, would come. Somebody would provide the strippers from somewhere. I never really understood how they kept getting new girls in there, but all these strippers would be dancing on the kitchen table as the guys kept throwing dollar bills at them. I didn't even know what the heck a strip club was; didn't know what the heck a stripper was; didn't know you were supposed to give them money like that. Well, I made less than seven bucks an hour; you do the math. How much money would I have for strippers after I'd just worked a four-hour shift? And the times when I worked a seven-hour shift, I started work at four o'clock and worked until 11 p.m., and had to catch an early bus to be at school the next morning by seven o'clock. So I didn't have a lot of time or money for strippers, although Marlon still owes me

$20 for one of the stripper-filled parties he threw at the house. But, hey, it's all good. I wrote that off as bad debt.

Around that time my insomnia started. I couldn't sleep because people were drinking and partying in the kitchen, and my room was twenty feet over. It was never an issue for Marlon; he was an adult. It seemed he planned the parties around his days off anyhow.

I was responsible for myself and whatever I was doing. I had no one to control me, the fact that I stayed out of trouble was completely my own doing. I'm sure a lot of people might want to take credit for my success, but they had nothing to do with it. I did that. I created the culture that I grew up in. I raised myself. I became my own mother, father and legal guardian. Anybody who claims otherwise, before, now, or ever in the future, is a liar. They are just trying to take credit for something that went right. I'm not a serial killer; I didn't become some kind of pervert or pedophile or deviant, and now they may want to take credit because people, especially my family members, love to take credit for things they didn't do. It makes them feel good and feeds their devious and evil souls.

I had a friend in high school who had come from Brooklyn to Bridgeport because he couldn't pass the official state test in New York to graduate high school. It was much easier to get a high school diploma in Connecticut — as long as you barely passed your courses, Connecticut pretty much handed them out in my opinion, especially if you went to one of the four public high schools there. He came to Connecticut to live with his sister, who lived right next to Bassick High School. His name was Petey. He pretended to be my friend until he graduated high school, but not before he had to go to summer school in 2004.

I've come to realize that Petey was never my friend for a few reasons: One, he had a car, a 1993 blue Honda Civic subcompact sedan. I didn't even have a bicycle. He never had enough money to put gas in his car, I had to help him with gas on many occasions. On another occasion, I had to lend him money to buy fancy, expensive rims for his car, which already had perfectly good ones. He wanted to show off to people who didn't matter; strangers he shouldn't need validation from. I helped him out, that was $200 I never got back. And the gas money, I never got back. But I still thought he was my friend for one reason — because I had no one else.

I thought he was one of my guys, that he was on my side, but not only did he use me for my money, he stole my girlfriend in the middle of it all. He used to give me a ride to go pick her up, and at times, he would go get her for me. Somewhere in the shuffle, he got her number and started seeing her. One time I called his sister's apartment at Fairfield Gardens and she informed me that he was busy in the room with my girlfriend. They were having sex in broad daylight. They betrayed me. I'm sure she fell for him because he spoke better English than I did and he had his own car.

He didn't have a need for my girlfriend because he had his own thing going on; he had many girls, way more than I did. He claimed he had lots of women in Connecticut and in Brooklyn, NYC where he'd resided for over a decade. But he took my girlfriend. When you are clearly a shady person that's what you do to someone you don't really consider a friend — take his girlfriend, because you've already taken everything else, his money, and his time.

Graduating high school was extremely difficult and I worked really hard to make that happen. Somehow I graduated, not only on time, but with extra credits, because throughout my junior and senior years I took many more classes than my peers. I worked during high school, first at Burger King and then at Price Rite. Both minimum-wage jobs where I had to work forever to get a ten-cent raise. And if they did give you a raise, the amount of work they required from you tripled, I didn't even want the raise.

I kept working hard; I even got second fastest cashier in a store contest. I'm sure they rigged it because there was no way the guy who won moved faster than I did. I had been determined to win that contest because I was still seeking validation from strangers. I needed that because I was missing the love and affection of a mother, a father, a sister — all the people who are supposed to provide you with unconditional love. I never got it. Even now, I'm still not receiving it.

I had nobody to invite to my high school graduation. I had four tickets but I couldn't find anyone who would come to see me graduate. My new stepmother, Shells, lived next door. She and I had grown close since I moved there; I spent a lot of time over at her house. I was close in age to her two sons and there was more to do at her place than at ours. Plus, she had DirecTV. Most of our meals were cooked at her place. Her gas was often shut off, so they mostly used the electric oven as a heat source; it would be turned on full blast with the door open during the winter months. Eddy, her youngest son, had figured out how to get free dial-up internet using 10-day or 14-day free trial offers. Companies such as Netscape and AOL would mail out free CDs offering a free trial of their internet service. Eddy became an expert at activating them and then cancelling before the trial period ended. Then he would use a different CD to get online and do the process all over again, flawlessly, for months. The CDs kept coming every week like clockwork, so he always had at least two or three unused CDs to scam with.

I was on the first floor; Shells was on the second. I gave her a ticket and she promised she would be there. She said, "I don't think I have to work that day; if I do, I'll get the shift covered." She was still working at the Walmart in Norwalk on Connecticut Avenue. She'd been working there for a while and she had to take as many buses as I did for my job at Burger King. Three.

She didn't show up for my graduation. She didn't care enough to.

I did, however, have one person who came. I'd given a ticket to Marlon, although he was the last person I expected to show up for me because the guy barely knew me. He was at least 40 years old and I was an 18-year-old student. He was more than twice my age and we didn't really share anything in common. We never talked about our personal philosophies or experiences. But Marlon was somehow there for me when nobody else in the entire world was. He kept his word and showed up in his 1992, gold Ford Taurus station wagon. I respected him for showing up for me, Baby Boy.

Yvette, Forgetful's social worker, took the only picture of me that day.

I had on the green cap and gown and Forgetful wore the white version of the same. At my heaviest, I barely weighed 120 pounds, soaking wet. I didn't look any better than when I first came to this country at seventeen years old, weighing 97 pounds. I wasn't only underweight, I was underweight by at least 30 or 40 pounds. Even when I got up to 125 or 130 pounds, I still looked hungry to the point where it was scary. My bones were protruding through my frail skin. My face was gaunt and my cheeks were sunken; my eyes receded inside my eye sockets.

Forgetful graduated the same day, but at least she had Ivette, her social worker, to take pictures. Ivette had been her social worker for over six months. This lady was directly responsible for her many moves to and from different foster homes all over the state.

That was pretty much it. I graduated high school and entered the real world. I had nothing. No money, no parents, no family, no material things — not that I wasn't used to that; I'd never had any, but it would have been nice to have had something or someone.

Over the years, I've paid many thousands of dollars to my family members, trying to buy their love, and trying to be there for each of them. I've cried many times, and literally begged them to; love me. Or show me what the heck all these other people that I know, are getting from their families. Why won't you love me? Why won't you help me? Why don't you care about me? No response.

Over three hundred million people live in this country, and I can't name three that I can honestly say have my back. I can give you a list of a hundred who took me for granted and used me, and I can give you a more specific list of five people who literally took me for everything I had, drained and bled me dry to the point where I now have less than twenty-five dollars in all my accounts combined. But I can't name three people that are "on my team."

I'm still experiencing the same pain, the same emotional emptiness inside. I'm still searching; I'm still lonely. The only difference is that now I have no money to give. I've tried and failed to buy the love of way too many people.

VERLY E. DOLCE

I failed because (I've just realized this) it's true that you can't buy real love. You can give people money and they'll give you their attention as long the money keeps flowing in. The minute it stops, is not coming as frequently or doesn't continuously increase, the love will also dissipate. With them, the money and love have a proportional relationship. I've found that when I continued to give someone money but the amount didn't increase, the love and the attention decreased. The illusion of respect for me also declined.

After finishing school, I started to make a couple of friends; again, people I thought were friends but weren't. They were opportunists looking for the next person to use. I was still way too naïve and inexperienced. I'd never had anyone to teach me or advise me. I never got "the talk" that parents give their children. Whatever talk you could think of, I never got it. I never got the stranger-danger talk or the sex talk. The only talk I ever got from my mother was when she told me what a failure I would be as soon as I made it to Babylon.

Those hurtful words that were the last declaration of my mother to me are still with me, although Red October told me, "Those were some of the most messed up things any mother could ever say to her son, but you need to prove her wrong."

I've been proving her wrong ever since. Do I think she regrets her words? No. I don't even think she remembers. It seems everyone develops amnesia, everyone. The bullies in my family have amnesia. The people who've used me have amnesia. The people whose burdens I am still carrying on my shoulders have amnesia. They placed their loads on my shoulders and kept walking as if they had nothing to do with it, and it was my issue in the first place. I am shouldering the weight of their wrongdoings while they are walking around free as a bird, free as a butterfly, continuing to pollinate, continuing to jump from flower to flower like their lives are perfect and they've never harmed anyone.

I don't think my mother remembers ninety-nine percent of the things she's ever done or said to me because they were never meant for me to remember. She continuously tried — and I'm going to have to say she failed — to beat me into submission and into giving up on life. She tried her best. And by "her best" I mean the tactics she used were straight slavery-era tactics. Slave owners used the most brutal forms of punishment to correct any perceived deficiencies in their slaves. Deficiencies may not have been deficiencies by other people's standards, but if the slave owner considered a behavior or attitude to be a deficiency and detrimental to the good order of the owner's plantation, they would beat the slave until they were completely submissive and their spirit was broken. They expected the slaves to eat out of the slave owner's hands like someone with an extreme case of Stockholm Syndrome.

That was what my own mother did to me. Now you tell why my mother is trying so hard to be my friend, as if she didn't do these things.

I don't know what the heck to say to this woman. I gave her money, but it was not enough. I've given her tens of thousands of dollars, two or three thousand at a time, still trying to buy her love. Love I should have gotten since 1985 for FREE. Because she's my mother. She brought me into this world. Her first kid. Unconditional love should have been given to me. But as far back as I can remember, I never had one moment when I felt like I had a loving mother. No, never. At least now I realize I can't afford to keep trying to buy her love. I'm done trying.

I don't want an abundance of parental hugs and kisses and affection at this moment because those times have passed. The time for my father to sit me down and teach me about life, that ship has sailed. The time for my father to teach me about the importance of maintaining a good credit score, how important financial independence is, the SAT in high school, picking the right college, picking the right college major, picking the right woman for me. The time for my mother to love and nurture me and protect me is gone. The sex talk. I never got it. Aren't you supposed to get it when you're a teenager? Telling your kid, "If you get a girlfriend, I'll kill you," is not the sex talk, Mother.

Making your son cover for you is not parenting, Father. Disowning your son because he refuses to continue to cover for you is not how a father is supposed to behave. Having ten kids with six different women is not building a family. It's the complete opposite of it as a matter of fact. I understand we all have our carnal desires and we all sometimes do things that might be a little bit outside of the box of what society condones. Father, I understand you're living outside the box, but you've been in way too many women's boxes, creating new humans and then abandoning them. If you're gonna live outside the box, at least be responsible for the offspring that come out of that box.

In 2002, right after the World Cup ended, when I was sixteen, I had to give my mother the sex talk. I had to sit her down, I explained to her that my father's intention was to impregnate her once more after which he would desert us again. I knew I needed to have the talk with her when I overheard him whispering his plans to her.

On June 30th 2002, Brazil won the World Cup hosted by South Korea and Japan. Outside of Brazil itself, Haiti has the most supportive pro-Brazil soccer fans. Ronaldo, full name Ronaldo Luís Nazário de Lima, scored eight goals for Brazil in seven games; he won the coveted golden boot for scoring the most goals in the tournament. Being a Brazil fan, Psychopath's plan was to name the new kid he was hoping for, Ronaldo. How did he know the baby would be a boy? I don't know but he was certain it would be. This guy didn't want the new kid; he wickedly wanted to spread his seed one more time.

Well, I disagreed with his enormously flawed logic. I stepped up and prevented his "Ronaldo" from happening. I had to. And I would do it all over again if I needed to.

I shouldn't have had to give my mother the sex talk. No, I shouldn't have had to sit my mother down and explain that it's a bad idea to even mingle with this guy who's here visiting you while he's still married, under a different name, to another woman in another country. I sat my mother down for a twenty-minute conversation in which I outlined the pros and cons of her getting pregnant again. At the end of the talk, I suggested birth control to her, and not only did I do that, I volunteered to be in charge of the birth control plan. I set a time for her to take her pills. I read up on it and then I put her on a schedule to prevent her getting pregnant for the fourth time by my loser psychopathic father. I engineered a plan to prevent my mother from going into further misery with what would have been a late pregnancy at 40 years old.

This was all happening during the time Forgetful and I were preparing to go to Babylon.

Psychopath came back a few months later and was furious that Surrogate wasn't pregnant. She couldn't explain to him what had happened. As far as I know, he still doesn't understand. He's clueless.

And why did Surrogate want to get married to her abuser? To be part of the choir, the married women's choir. She badly wanted to be baptized into some man made religion — though there's no such thing as a religion that isn't stained. They're all stained with the blood of indigenous peoples, their own people, people of other faiths. They'll murder their own people as soon as the person changes his/her views, refuses to buy in their nut job propaganda, or refuses to give them money. Money they need to further spread their message of unconditional hatred around the globe.

* * *

I tried college, but couldn't do it because I had way too much going on with work, and my sleep disorder was worsening. I would try to fall asleep but couldn't. My friend Angel tried to help out by giving me a ride to school with him, but that meant I'd have to leave earlier. Sometimes I'd miss twenty minutes or so of class or I wasn't able to make it at all. My first two college semesters were a disaster. I had a GPA of 0.67 on a four-point scale. Even students who nearly failed the class with a D grade had at least a 1.5 GPA. It wasn't that I failed most of my classes; I couldn't wake up to show up. I got mostly Fs, and I was able to properly withdraw from only one class. And then, I don't know why but for some reason I signed up for Advanced Spanish. And that was a failure. Just to summarize, it was terrible. I felt a kind of misery I wouldn't wish on anyone, not even my worst enemy.

I started working at RadioShack, a company that has since closed most of its stores due to competition from online sales and, in my opinion also because they were overcharging people: a six-foot cable cost around $18 and an eight-foot coaxial cable around $22, approximately twice what they cost elsewhere. Of course, you can get those online now for a couple of dollars. Amazon wasn't very big or well-known yet. The early 2000s brought in the internet revolution, and the electronics stores started to diminish little by little. I left RadioShack in 2007.

I still didn't have a car while I was working there, but within a year of when I first started, I was working in seven different stores. Whenever they needed coverage I would volunteer. This meant I had to take the bus to many different locations. Once when it was snowing and I couldn't get a bus, I took a taxi from Bridgeport to work a four-hour shift in Westport. I paid $55 for the taxi and at $6.90 an hour, I made less than $30 bucks before taxes. Being a single guy with no dependents put me in the worst tax bracket. Essentially, I paid the government and the company at least $30 for allowing me to work that day.

I eventually found a permanent spot at a Radio Shack in Fairfield, not far from the Shop Rite. The most memorable experiences there were several homosexually-charged sexual assaults that I almost fell victim to. The store manager, Adam, was chronically high on various drugs. He confessed to me that for a time he had used crack cocaine, and that once in a while he would still indulge in some kind of hard drugs. But alcohol was his thing when I met him. He smoked and drank a lot. Drinking and driving seemed to be his favorite hobby.

This was in 2005 and I still didn't have a car. Adam had a white pickup truck and he would offer me and other employees rides. I noticed that the other male employees never accepted a ride from him, but I couldn't figure out why. Hey, it's a free ride, why won't you jump on?

I did think it was a little odd because he was going to New Haven and we were in Fairfield, it was out of his way. But I was still new to the country so

I thought, I don't really know this guy and he's offering to drive me though it's out of his way, but maybe this is how people are here. I thought he wanted to be friends. This continued for a few months. He'd pick me up, we'd hang out, and sometimes he'd come over and bring beer. I never drank; he'd drink all the beer and then drive home. I guess he was a lucky drunk driver because he never got into an accident. Not that anyone should do it, but this guy somehow mastered it.

This went on until one day he called the store when I was working and said he was in the area and asked if he could give me a ride. He also asked another guy, Sean if he wanted a ride, and Sean told him, "No, no, I don't want a ride, I'm taking the bus." I thought it was odd that he'd prefer to ride the bus, but I went with Adam, and when he dropped me off at home he came in to hang out for a while. At that time I was renting a room for $350 a month because I couldn't afford anything more. I had Dish Network and we were watching Family Guy, a very funny cartoon show that aired on Fox. Sean had introduced me to the show, which had been running for twenty years; it was cancelled once but got put back on. The program still hasn't won an Emmy, and I'm sure they really want one because all the other long running comedy shows have at least one.

I spaced out, I was enjoying the program when out of nowhere he leaned over and grabbed my crotch and wouldn't let go. I exclaimed, "What the heck are you doing?!" He opened his mouth and stuck his tongue out and waggled it and started making sucking noises. I was shocked! What the heck is this?! You gotta be kidding me! Thank god I was wearing long pants, and had a belt on and my shirt tucked in, which made it more difficult for him, but he still would not let go. I had to fight this guy off. It took two or three minutes of serious struggling but I finally got him off of me. I jumped up and said, "You know what, get out of here! You gotta leave right now." But then what did I do? I walked him to his car. I'd survived a potential sexual assault by the dude and I walked him to his car? He got in his car and I told him to go. We lost touch when I was transferred to another store.

VERLY E. DOLCE

Later, thinking back, I realized that Adam had been buttering me up, hoping to have sex with me. I had thought we were cool, but he had an ulterior motive all along, and I think everybody but me knew it. I was still too naïve. I'm not homophobic; I'm not gay. I wasn't trying to flirt with him. I'm nice to everybody. I think it's important to say hi and be friendly to people. For heaven's sake, the national fruit of my country is the pineapple. It's literally the oldest known symbol of hospitality. It's a welcoming symbol; I'm a welcoming guy. An extrovert if you will.

When I got back to work and I told Sean about my experience, he said, "Oh yeah, I thought you knew." I said, "Wait, what do you mean?" He replied, "Yeah, this guy was clearly gay. He was making attempts on you; he tried to hit on us; that's why we didn't take his rides."

Another coworker, Chris, seconded what Sean said. I felt like a fool. I didn't know I'd been putting out a "come sexually assault me vibe." Adam had been sizing me up to see if he could do stuff with me sexually. What did I do? I guess I led him on. I must have given him some kind of signal that made him think things were okay; maybe it was because I didn't refuse his rides like the other guys did. I will never know.

Around the same time, another guy came into the store to buy a cell phone. Cell phones were the hot items we were supposed to upsell. Our manager, Howard, would call in when he was off to ask how many we'd sold that day. I had the utmost respect for Howard; he was a bit older and full of wisdom. He had a noticeable limp. He was a retired owner of a Saab dealership, he was managing at Radio Shack to pass the time during his retirement.

Suddenly, a customer came in to buy a phone, and both Sean and I helped him. We had similar schedules and we worked well together. Sean was a really nice guy; he seemed able to read people in a way I couldn't, and he didn't make my mistake of being too nice to unsuspected homosexual predators.

The guy wanted a phone and we sold him one. I don't remember if it was me or Sean who rang up the sale, but we both helped the guy, whose name was Jeff. Before Jeff left, he asked me, "Oh yeah, can I have your number?" I was a young kid, 19 years old, and this guy seemed to be 40-something; he was for sure not in his thirties. But, still naïve, I thought, How nice, new people. Let me give my number to this nice gentleman…

Same thing happened again. Sometimes Jeff would pick me up at my house and we'd go to his house and hang out for a little bit. The one weird thing I noticed was that every time we hung out, he always had someone to pick up from the Fairfield train station. They were always boys, my age or much younger. They were definitely not in their twenties, and I highly doubt half of them were even 18 years old. He told me they were his young cousins and nephews from New York. I believed him; I thought to myself, this guy sure has a lot of little cousins and nephews. I did notice that the boys never seemed happy to see him. They were never smiling like I was. I never saw anything happen and I never inquired. I always said I had to go home and left. I'm guessing Jeff was importing these boys from New York City, or wherever his preferred hunting grounds were, to the small train station at Fairfield, and then he'd put them up in a room.

For a time I lived near to him, on the street where the Haitian church was in the Black Rock area of Bridgeport, right before the Bridgeport-Fairfield line.

One time he had a very effeminate gentleman with him; he wore a lot of make-up, including eyeliner and shadow and his eyebrows were done in the style popular today, thick and well-traced. Although he had a masculine body, he had a very feminine voice and mannerisms, and his face and voice didn't match. The guy was giving me dirty looks and at first I didn't understand why, but then I realized he probably thought I was competition for Jeff. Jeff was certainly the type that loved to have multiple partners because he was hitting on me, although I didn't know it at the time.

The last time I went to his house we were talking about music and other stuff. I told him about my unhappy college experience: "Hey man, I just had a terrible semester and a half of college and things didn't work out. It was not good." Jeff told me he knew someone in the choir at Michigan State University, and if I wanted to get in, I would be pretty much a shoo-in in terms of admissions. I felt he understood that I wanted to go back to school and wanted to help me out. Until he asked me, "Hey, do you play the skin flute?" I didn't understand this weird question, so I said, "No, I don't know what that is."

I didn't get it until a year later when I asked my friend from Sudan, Vanessa (with the body of Beyonce), what a skin flute was. She said, "Wait, are you serious?" I said, "I don't know what that is, what is it?" She said, "It is exactly what it sounds like, a skin flute. Imagine the male body, the male sexual organ that looks like a flute. I can't believe you didn't get this. It's literally in the name, a flute that has a skin on it, or an organ that looks like a flute."

Belatedly, I realized what Jeff had asked me. I hadn't had a clue.

After I stopped hanging out with both Adam and Jeff, I was transferred to another store at the Westfield Mall in Trumbull. My transportation issue eased somewhat because I only had to take one bus and I didn't have to go through the whole ordeal of going downtown first and then taking a second bus from downtown Bridgeport to Fairfield.

Shortly after I moved to the Trumbull store, I was taking the city bus to work in Trumbull and I recognized a guy from high school. I remembered Tyshon because he was very effeminate and he'd had a tough time at school. Back then, transgender people were not allowed to use the restroom of their choice. Whenever he'd go into the boys' bathroom, he would get dirty looks and lewd comments. Guys would make fun of him, push him, call him names and humiliate him. I never did this. My grandmother had taught me better. I would never treat another human in such a manner regardless of their sexual orientation, ethnicity, or how they identified. I carried myself the way I knew she would want me to, like a proper young man.

Tyshon got on the bus and sat down next to me. He said, "I remember you from high school." I thought, Yeah, we just graduated a couple of years ago. Then he proceeded to tell me about his apartment, how he had a nice place of his own and that he had a big bed. I responded something like,

"Okay, cool, all right." He told me he worked at Victoria's Secret, which I thought was weird. When we got to the mall, I got off the bus first, he walked really fast to get in front of me. It seemed he wanted me to notice that the rear area of his extremely tight women's jeans, they were ripped all over and seemed too tight around the butt to be men's, the buttocks were completely cut off to reveal women's lacy panties. I thought, What the heck? He half-turned with a little smirk and waved his hand, saying "Okay, byeee, see ya!."

I mentioned this incident to Goldie once and she said, "Obviously, he was telling you that he had his own place because he wanted you to come over." I realized she was right and wondered, Why does this keep happening to me? I wish I could tell you that was the last time I got hit on by dudes, but no, these encounters continued. There were at least five more over a three- to four-year timespan. One was with Jack, a cook at the Uno's Pizzeria I was working at in Fairfield. This was in 2009. We were at work when he asked me, in a very feminine voice, "Oh, hey, Verly do you burn?" Do I burn? I took a guess that was lingo for smoking weed and for whatever reason he wanted us to chill and smoke weed together.

I have never done any illegal drugs. The only drugs I've ever put in my mouth were prescribed to me. I didn't go burn with this guy. But someone clued me in that Jack had also been flirting with me. I'd wondered why he was speaking in that feminine voice, flapping his eyelashes, and turning around like he was a princess or something. Just weird, man, just weird.

I worked at a different franchise of that same pizzeria about a year and a half later in Milford. A coworker, this dude was big and he was tall. He also worked the carnivals whenever they'd come to town, and eventually he left the server job at the pizzeria to go be a full-time carnie, going wherever the carnival went. He was a nice guy, but one day at work, he said flirtatiously to me, "Oh, you already have me against the wall and we just met." What the f---?

I think I'm just too nice, and some people interpret my kindness as flirtatiousness. It had never occurred to me that giving out my number to random people could lead to me almost getting sexually assaulted by one guy and propositioned by another. I don't have any homosexual desires. I never did. I wholeheartedly have a strong desire to treat everyone equally regardless of whatever, whoever they are.

I need to be a bigger jerk, not to gays specifically, to everyone, so people will stop taking advantage of me, because this has been going on my entire life and I am tired of it.

I am tired of feeling lonely, tired of being alone, and having nobody in my corner, while at the same time that I'm feeling so despondent, other people are telling me how much I have helped them and thanking me for all I have done for them. I also know many family members who should be telling me this; instead, they are ungrateful and still asking more from me, as if I've never done anything for them. People ask to borrow money; I give it to them. When it's time to pay me back, it seems they never have more than ten percent of it. Oftentimes, I just let it go. I estimate that I have more than fifty thousand dollars in outstanding bad debts that I have written off as money I'm never going to get back.

There was the fat guy in Bridgeport who was illegal, couldn't even get a phone under his name. His name was Wilkes. I got him a phone from T-Mobile. He ran up the bill to over five hundred bucks by buying way too many ringtones and ring back tones. I'm pretty sure those things are obsolete now, they cost around three dollars each back then. When I asked him about paying his bill, he took the phone, threw it in my face, and told me to go screw myself and go screw my mother. Obviously I didn't continue to help that guy. But you know what, I'm not worried about him. I'm sure the universe made him pay.

Then there was that chick, her name was CeCe. We were dating and I got her a phone through Cingular Wireless, now AT&T, with my employee discount while I was working at RadioShack in the Trumbull mall. She lived in Brooklyn, and was talking daily to a married dude in Florida, using the phone that I was paying for. When I got the phone bill, I saw that ninety-nine percent of her phone calls and text messages were to this fool in Florida. I'm pretty sure he lived in the greater Miami area. Either Miami or Fort Lauderdale; it's all crap. Florida's crap. She ran up that bill to over eight hundred dollars, then told me she needed to go move in with her aunt, who was sick. She moved in with the guy in Florida, then mailed me back the phone. After two months of lies, she finally came clean and admitted she had moved in with another guy, who had three kids and a wife. CeCe, I'm not claiming to be a saint, but you left me, a single guy, to go move in with a married man with three kids? While the single guy is paying for your phone? Another unfavorable incidence I suffered.

You name it, whatever situation in life you can think of, I have an experience where someone used, misused, or abused me to the extreme, from parents and siblings to strangers, to friends. Even the people I thought were closest to me, they've all somehow gotten a leg up on me. Is that going to destroy my faith in humanity? No. I'm not gonna let these people do that to me.

Have I stopped flirting with gays? Yes, I have. If I see a guy coming and I don't know what he wants, I no longer smile and greet him with open arms. I learned my lesson. Not again.

To finish up this homosexual theme, a couple of months ago, I moved into a new place in the San Fernando Valley. I went shopping at the nearby Northridge Fashion Center. Another customer started chatting with me about the store we were in.

"I know, it's a nice store; they have my size now since I lost nearly fifty pounds," I told him as the reason I now wear a size small shirt and 30x32 pants. He was talking in an overly feminine voice, the way Jack had ten years earlier. I was thinking he might be gay, but he confused me because he kept talking about his girlfriend. I didn't say anything but I was thinking, This guy has a girlfriend? He sounds like a girl.

He followed me out as I was leaving the mall and caught up to me, chatting about this or that, and then he said, "Oh, my god, I've got to get your number; I hardly ever connect with people like this. This never happens." Guess what I did? Yeah. I gave the guy my phone number. What is wrong with me?

Later, Mrs. Nordhal, a friend's mother, explained that the girlfriend talk was to let me know that he could be the girlfriend in the relationship. I did it again. I flirted with yet another gay fellow.

I'm done. No more giving my phone number out to guys. I'm not giving my phone number out to anyone until I can be sure of their intentions. Only if we have business together or we have a specific reason for you to be asking me for my phone number will it be given to you. That way, I can be sure I will not be sexually pursued by more random dudes. That's my declaration, because I am beyond tired of it.

A couple of the incidents were scary. I was underage when Adam assaulted me, I didn't drink, but if I had been drinking, I don't know what would have happened because he was violently trying to get to my junk. Yeah, I'm done.

- Goldie -

I left Bohio in 2002, and shortly after I graduated high school in 2004, I met Goldie. I was working at Radio Shack and she worked at J.C. Penney's in the same mall. From the get-go something seemed oddly familiar about her, but I couldn't really put my finger on it. I said something that I meant as a compliment. I casually told her, "You're kinda cute."

Making a comment about her physical appearance was typical for me because, quite frankly, I never took the time to get to know any females on an intellectual or emotional level, nor did I want to. My interest in women was strictly physical, because at that time I was following, although subconsciously, in Psychopath's footsteps, and my goal was to have meaningless sex with as many women as possible. I had no regard, true feelings or emotions toward any of my partners; it was just sex. I believed sex would ease the emotional pain and sorrow of my traumas and disappointments in life. It did, but only for a short time. As anyone who's having recreational sex will tell you, it really does not mean anything. As soon as it was over, all the negative feelings came crashing back — all the pain, anger, frustration, feelings of worthlessness, uselessness, despair that I hadn't accomplished anything and that my life was meaningless. I didn't know it then, but I was trying to fill a void that was created in my earliest years by having no one to fulfill my most basic needs.

Instinctually, Goldie must have sensed that I didn't have any money or potential to acquire it because she made it clear she wasn't interested. She was looking for someone to rescue her from her current situation, someone, I would later learn, who could continuously pump money into her forever-deepening money pit. She ignored me; didn't return my call.

Of course I was attracted to Goldie. Of course she was familiar. She is also a sociopath. Similarly to someone suffering from Stockholm syndrome, I craved more and more of that familiar dysfunction. Her rejections felt right. It reminded me of the first seventeen years of my life. It was wrong. But it felt like exactly what I needed because it was what I knew. What I grew up with.

But to get back to our story, Goldie and I met; she rejected me, and we went our separate ways. That should have been the end of the story, but a year and a half later, I did something regrettable. I called her store and asked to speak to her. I had gotten my driver's license and bought a car and I was hoping she still hadn't done so. She hadn't, so I offered her a ride home. She agreed.

She got off work at 7:00 p.m. That frigid, breezy night, I was waiting for her in my new-to-me Camry. It wasn't the best car, not flashy or new. It was old and beat up, a red 1986 Toyota Camry Deluxe Edition with over 150,000 miles on it. My good friend Jimmy had sold me the car after teaching me to drive in it. I paid him hardly anything for the lessons and he sold me the car for only $650. Although it was cheap, I still didn't have enough money left to pay for it after buying insurance and paying the registration and taxes. In Connecticut these fees were very high, especially given my very low income at the time. Jimmy gave me the car with only a verbal agreement that I would pay him later, I did.

I drove Goldie home but it was another false start. I'd lost my cell phone prior; I lost her number. Another year and a half passed before I saw her again.

I had just returned from my first trip back to Bohio to visit family. I was preparing to start culinary school at Lincoln Tech in Shelton, Connecticut, and I was on my way to the barbershop. I wanted to look good for school. I glanced over at the bus stop for the line that goes up to Main Street, and there was Goldie waiting for the bus. I was surprised that she apparently still didn't have a driver's license or car.

I drove on for about half a mile, fighting the urge to turn around. I experienced what felt like the proverbial devil and angel on my shoulders.

The angel: "Don't do it; she's crazy." The devil: "What's the worst that can happen? You may get laid, and then you can move on."

There was no way I could have known that Goldie would become my worst nightmare.

The Devil won. I made a U-turn and pulled up, noticing she seemed happy to see me. Goldie got in, and then she told me that she was hungry. A red flag, but I was focused on getting laid, so I took her to lunch. We went to a place called Friendly's that was supposed to be an affordable family place. It was on Main Street, right across from the armed forces recruiting center and behind the food-poisoning-establishment known as Red Lobster.

I was hoping she'd order something inexpensive, but she ordered so much food that I only had enough money to get myself a side of onion rings. She had two bags of take out food to take home. She essentially crippled me financially with that unplanned extravagance. I had to borrow forty bucks from my friend Bob Le Highest to pay my rent later that month. I didn't tell him why I was short on my rent but I made sure to pay him back from my next paycheck.

Shortly after this, Goldie and I started dating. By dating, I mean me taking her out and letting her buy whatever the heck she wanted. She loved the "2 for $20" deal at Chili's. It was not too bad, although the food was salty at times. We'd typically go to a few different restaurants and have a few drinks. Our dates usually cost me fifty or sixty bucks including tip, an entire day's pay. I tried really hard to impress her but she was unimpressible. Could not be impressed no matter what I did. I kept trying. Every time I'd go out with her I couldn't afford to do anything else for at least a week.

We started going out more, and a short time later she became my girlfriend. Soon after, Goldie demanded I call every female-sounding name in my contacts and inform them that I had a girlfriend now and our friendship couldn't continue because she forbade it. I obliged, except for one. Carpe Diem. When she discovered this disobedience, Goldie punched me in the face right in front of her two obese cousins, who easily weighed over 300 pounds each. That was the first of many physical assaults by Goldie.

* * *

A year or so after we started dating, Surrogate came to Babylon to live. Forgetful was pregnant, and finding she'd bitten off more than she could chew with that uncalculated development, she applied to bring Surrogate to help with her impending childbirth. Forgetful wanted the type of cheap labor only a close family member can provide nowadays. She was about to marry a first-grade loser — with many college degrees but extremely uneducated — clearly not a marriage material kind of guy, of which I informed Forgetful, and advised her not to marry him. Her response was to uninvite me to the wedding.

Forgetful had personally uninvited me, and her man had also told her not to hang out with me because I was not a good influence in their relationship, yet I still had to not only attend, but walk her down the aisle because Surrogate insisted that I do this. Forgetful had wanted Gene, one of Surrogate's younger brothers, to walk her down the aisle, but he had flaked at the last minute. I agreed to do it because I was still trying to please everyone.

Forgetful has since divorced that husband. He is still as horrible a person as he was when she first met him. He's a wannabe pastor, a false Prophet. I was told, he holds an online Ph.D. in Theology. I guess for a long time she didn't see him for the hot mess that he was. When she finally filed for divorce, Forgetful complained that nobody was helping her and nobody had told her not to marry the loser. I know that she can honestly say that to herself because she always forgets anything people do for her and she never remembers anything she ever does wrong. She remembers only the wrongs people do to her and believes nobody has ever had her back. But I promise you the opposite is true. She has done everything she could to piss people off, take from them, and in turn, make everything all about her. She's so overly consumed with herself that she doesn't see how terrible she's treated everyone else. That's Forgetful for you. My lovely little sister.

Surrogate came to visit me and Goldie, and right away the two of them did not get along. I believe the biggest reason was that when they saw each other it was like looking in the mirror. This is when I began to realize they were the same person. I saw no difference between them — two terrible people, horrible to one another and to everyone else.

To be honest, most of the time I found their fights very intriguing. Surrogate and Goldie were constantly mimicking each other, saying the same exact thing back and forth. It was almost like watching someone with multiple personality disorder arguing with herself.

The next time they were together was May 2012 when I graduated from Norwalk Community College. It appeared, Goldie and Surrogate could not be in the same place and act like civilized people. The moment they saw each other, they resumed fighting. The fights were upsetting for everyone except me; I found them wildly entertaining. Their fight at Norwalk Community College was witnessed by my friend Nae and her daughter Nadie, and it sent them major red flags about Goldie. They were embarrassed for Goldie and felt sorry for me. Bob Le Highest was also there and he too couldn't believe the level of selfishness being displayed. I didn't see it that way.

As for myself and the way they treated me, how do I put this? A doormat gets more respect than I ever did from either of those two women. Seeing them together helped me recognize that these were not the best relationships for me. They weren't good for my peace of mind. Awareness was the first step, but it would be many more years before I was able to act on the knowledge and completely remove them from my life.

***

Shortly before our two-year dating anniversary, I was passing the time in Goldie's living room before driving to NCC. My phone rang and I chose not to answer it. It was a female friend whom I had no romantic relationship with, but I didn't feel like reciting the "I have a girlfriend now" monologue to her. Goldie grabbed me by my collar and wouldn't let go. She was hitting me vigorously, especially in the face. I finally got free and attempted to leave her house. She grabbed a bottle of liquid bleach from the top of her washing machine and emptied it over my head, screaming obscenities. The bleach got into my eyes and blinded me. I frantically felt my way to the kitchen sink, using the wall to navigate, desperate to flush my eyes with water. Just as I touched the sink, I felt a stunning blow on the back of my head. I put my head under the faucet and ran water into my eyes, praying my sight would return. I heard Goldie's footsteps pounding upstairs to her jail-cell-sized room. I could see again. I finished washing my face and went into the living room where her grandmother had witnessed the entire altercation. She said nothing. I went back home to change clothes because I smelled putrid and my outfit was ruined. My brand-new book bag was also destroyed.

  I stayed with her, but the abuse didn't stop; it intensified. About a year before joining the Navy, I moved to the finished attic of my high school friend SJ's father's house. During one of our heated arguments there, Goldie punched me in the neck. I left the room because I couldn't stand her presence for one more second. In retaliation for me walking away from her, she poured her bottle of water all over my TV, DVD player and cable box, then she left. I had to call my friend Nae to come and help me deal with that craziness. When Nae and I saw the extent of the damage to my electronics, we were both speechless. Nae looked at me with a concerned look on her face; I missed the cue. I didn't end the dysfunctional relationship; I dug in deeper. I was unaffected and clearly very blind then.

  She routinely stalked me at that house and at the place I lived before that, a basement apartment. I could clearly tell when she was stalking me there, almost always. At the time, she drove a 1994 Navy blue Lexus ES300 that I'd helped her buy. The car was uniquely loud due to multiple holes in the muffler and a catalytic converter problem. I recognized the unmistakable sound of her engine outside my house at least once a day whenever we weren't talking. I would often look out in time to see her license plate as she was turning the corner. That sound was very fitting for her psychotic behavior and personality.

For one reason or another, I found her unpredictable behavior sexy back then. I only saw the cuteness and not the erraticness in her actions. I thought she really loved me and that was why she continuously invaded my privacy or treated me like trash. I thought her love for me was so strong, it drove her to the brink of insanity. She was NOT a mother. I avoided getting her pregnant. Nonetheless, I was required to hand her presents for eight of the ten mother's days we spent together. I should say, obligated to or else. The "or else" part came in the form of physical blows, psychological torture, emotional detachment and everything in between. She carried out her total war against me for over a decade.

- Boot Camp -

I graduated college, and was scheduled to be shipped out at the end of August. When the time came, I reported to the Naval Base at Great Lakes, Illinois via Chicago's O'Hare International Airport.

From the very first day, things took a turn for the worse. Our recruit division commander (RDC), an extremely hairy guy with a huge unibrow, who considered himself a real hotshot chief, spat on me, punched me in the chest, and pushed me. This was his response to my asking a question regarding the shaving procedure. I knew from disastrous past experiences that due to my very sensitive skin I was unable to shave with straight razors. When I asked if I could use an alternative type of razor, he lost it, and threatened me, "I will make sure that you don't stick around long! Mark my words, you will NOT graduate with this division!" I did. Although every day thereafter, things continued to deteriorate.

After our initial encounter the RDC really had it in for me. I believe he was European, possibly Greek or Turkish. He acted as if the entire universe revolved around him. This guy really thought that he was IT. I couldn't disagree more but what was I gonna do? I was a new recruit and he was some kind of star who was fast-tracked to chief in less than nine years, and he did not let us forget it. Almost daily he bragged about how he was a hotshot of some sort.

From the time I got there everything was terrible and kept getting worse. There was a lot of hurrying up and waiting. From being woken up on the first morning and rushed to breakfast, having to shovel food down our throats within a few minutes, then run upstairs for the "pump and dump" (use your imagination) for which we were allowed around two minutes, so we could hurry back to the berthing area where we had absolutely nothing for three straight hours. It was senseless. We could have done something useful with our time, but we couldn't because we didn't have permission to use the restroom for more than a few seconds.

For me to say that boot camp was extremely hard and almost unbearable would be an understatement. There was a lot of homosexual activity. We've already established that I'm not against homosexuals; I didn't know that was an active thing in the military. But apparently, when you put too many guys together and there's no women around, that happens.

Actually, there were women around. We had a sister division, which is often the case. Our division number was 352 and our sister division was 351. Each division is assigned an RDC. The RDCs are typically given one or two E-5, or second-class petty officers to work with. The divisions operate together so they did everything in parallel. The divisions were berthed across from one another.

I'm not an expert on women or their looks, but these women did not look their best. After chopping off their hair, taking off their fake eyelashes and makeup — lipstick, concealer, foundation, eye shadow — everything women use to enhance their true beauty, or not so true beauty, was gone. They were really unattractive. And their hygiene wasn't the best, either. I highly doubt some of them brushed their teeth on a regular basis, or if they did, I don't think they did such a good job because their teeth looked hideous. Out of fifty females, Blake, a tall brunette, the only one who remained cute despite it all.

I guess at some point the guys looked across the hallway and saw the women; they looked back and saw the men, and some of them were like, "You know what, I'm gonna take my chances in here."

That was boot camp. At least the first few weeks. Eventually the shaving situation was resolved. They saw that my face was bleeding and literally falling apart from the razors bumps, they were compelled into giving me a break from shaving.

During this entire time, I was dating Goldie but we rarely talked. For the first few weeks of boot camp I kept missing her whenever I'd try to call. I knew she wasn't really busy, at least not work-wise; she never had time for me. I ended up sending her a letter that was less than kind, not a nice letter at all.

It was very rude; it was very mean; it was coming from a really, really tough place. I had absolutely no one. I wasn't dating anyone in my division, nor was I interested in either males or females at the time because, after all, I had a girlfriend back in Connecticut. It was upsetting, so I sent the awful letter. I sent over twenty-five loving letters; that was the only negative one, she did use that letter against me later. That's the only one she used because that's the one that painted me in a negative light. Goldie is all about making me look like a bad person so she can look like an innocent victim. In reality, she was a gold-digging opportunist who took advantage of me, giving absolutely nothing in return for me giving her a better life. She took and took but gave back nothing.

Finally boot camp was almost over, and graduation was scheduled for 10 a.m., November 2, 2012. About a week prior, the one person in life I ever truly loved, my grandmother, passed away. No one told me she was gone. Goldie, her grandmother and Surrogate decided that it wasn't the best idea to let me know that my dear grandmother had passed. Their rationale? They claimed they didn't want to interfere with my training. Screw the training. Screw the job. She was my world, my everything, the most important person in my life. Everyone knew it. They saw the situation through their opportunistic goggles and selfishly decided not to inform me she was no longer inhabiting an Earthly vessel. They wouldn't benefit financially if I didn't graduate from boot camp.

Had I known, I might have been able to get a pass so I could grieve, at least pay my final respects to the one person who mattered the most to me. That was not fair. They took it upon themselves to come up with the perfect excuse not to tell me. By the time I learned she was gone, it was too late. Her funeral was held on the morning of November 3rd, and they told me the news at noon on November 2nd. I tried to get an emergency pass but the timing was terrible because everyone was focused on graduation. I wasn't able to go. The time for any meaningful action had passed.

Grandma Rose passed away in late October of 2012. In her final days, she was staying near my aunt Carmen's house. Carmen was by her bedside, she clearly and vividly remembers my grandma asking for one person, saying she didn't want to go without seeing me one last time. This woman had many other people she could have asked for to be there for her as a dying wish. She asked for me; she told them to contact me and let me know she was ready to go, but not before we talked so she could tell me one last time how much she loved me. Her pleas fell on deaf ears; no one told me, and just like that, she passed to the other not-always-visible realm.

    I didn't know it at the time, but I felt it all the way in Great Lakes, Illinois, thousands of miles away from her. I'd felt it that entire week. I felt out of place in the world. Telepathically, she sent me the message and I received it. I felt an unfillable void inside, and on the day of my graduation from boot camp on November 2, 2012, around 8 a.m., before I got the news, I couldn't breathe; I felt like my heart was about to stop, as if a part of me had physically died.

    The last time I saw my grandma was in 2009 when I made my first visit back to Bohio. She was the very first person I went to see. To be frank, she was the reason I went back there in the first place. When I had last spoken to her over the phone, I knew that she understood how tough life was for me. Before the phone was taken away from her, in the three-minute conversation we had, she told me over fifty times how much she loved me. She wanted me to remember that because her love for me was limitless and eternal. She said to me, "SonSonn, wap kitem mouri anvan ou antre?" Loosely translated: "Are you going to let me die before you come back home?"

    On March 31st of 2009, I landed in Cap-Haitien. The next day, I saw her. She was very skinny and had some medical issues, but her face lit up when she saw me, as did mine. We went down to the photography studio, Kanpela, to take a few pictures to commemorate this epic moment. Our reconnection. We talked and she went home. Over the next week and a half, I stopped by to see her regularly, over the displeasures of many. I didn't care, she was my world and I didn't worry about other people's objections.

    It has always seemed crazy to me that Grandma Rose was Surrogate's mother; they were opposites in every way. Surrogate never liked her mother, partly because Grandma Rose threatened to "whip her butt" if she mistreated me. She preferred her father, who didn't care for me. In 1999, things got so bad for me that I escaped to go live with my grandma that summer. The abuse was too much, and scars were crisscrossing my body with Surrogate's successful efforts to brand me over and over, like a steer.

Surrogate was a spoiled and ungrateful daughter who never appreciated anything my dear grandmother did for her. Rose always had my back. She was the only person who ever made me feel valued, wanted, needed; that I mattered and was important in this life. In the toughest of times, when Surrogate would do her utmost to make sure my life was unlivable — as if she wished my entire existence to be washed away and wiped away from the face of the earth — I found solace in knowing that I could talk to my grandmother and she would make everything better. She always did. She was awesome.

On November second of two thousand twelve, the day of graduation, they told me to sit down because they had something to tell me. Since then, if anybody ever tells me, "I've got something to tell you, please sit down," I immediately get really upset. I'm still grieving. I never got the time to grieve. I never had a chance to say goodbye to my beloved grandmother because these people came together and decided to deprive me of this.

* * *

The only person in my entire life who's ever shown me love and had my back is no longer with us; however, I know she is still looking down and protecting me every day. My dear grandmother is the very definition of what a mother is. If Mother Earth were to take a break, my grandma could step in and do as good of a job of protecting all the inhabitants of the planet. She would do it the same way nature does, because she's a wonderful person, the smartest person I've ever met. If I could bring her back, for even one hour, day or one week, I would give up my life so that she could live for that one day or that one week. For I know in that one hour, one day, or one week that she was here, she would positively impact the lives of so many more people than I ever could.

I still see her as clear as day. Thanks to her, my premonitions have been nothing short of magical and powerful. I'm now more spiritually awakened than ever. I'm not a prophet or a voodoo priest; I'm simply a humble African man with a special relationship that helps guide me down the right paths. I no longer have a bunch of scary déjà-vu experiences, I now call them guiding light moments. I embrace them with open arms and open mind because my grandma wants me to know she is STILL looking out for me. I see her in my dreams at least once a year and she always appears when things are the toughest for me, just like old times.

Grandma, I love you. I miss you. And until my final moment here, I will never stop spreading your message of love and acceptance all over the world.

- Mississippi -

On top of not being able to go back to Bohio to attend Grandma's funeral, I had to report that morning to quite possibly the worst military base in the world. I'll give you a hint. It's in Meridian, Mississippi. At the horror-movie-set-like Naval Air Station in "SEXY" Meridian. The only thing to do there was getting in trouble out in town. That's it.

Mississippi is an awful state, a terrible place. About a week before I went to boot camp, I happened to read an article about how Mississippi is one of the few states in the Union where one race is still chasing another race (that is possibly a minority) with cars, trying to kill them because they still hate the fact that "those people" exist in their country or in their territory. Mississippi. Don't ever go there. I have nothing against you, Mississippi. I'm unconvinced you're a tourist hot spot. Or a spot for anything. I also heard from a few sailors: the town of Meridian was depressing, the attractions are lame, the women are huge, the restaurants and bars are tiny. Nope, not for me. I'm good. Let me just say going to Mississippi did not make things better. When I got there, I learned that somebody had called ahead and warned them to keep an eye on me because I was unhappy that I hadn't been able to go on leave. That hairy Chief with the massive unibrow did. He found a way to continue to torment me even after I had narrowly escaped his slimy paws.

The training facility had obviously been built in the 1930s or '40s. It for sure was at least sixty or seventy years old. And the classrooms were aesthetically weird and poorly designed. Everything felt like it was back in the World War Two era. Maybe between World War One and Two. That was the vibe throughout the entire area, the entire base. Needless to say, a lot of people got in trouble for drinking and doing all kinds of reckless stuff because there was absolutely nothing to do besides that. Nothing.

I did not have a great time in Mississippi. To put it in perspective, I was in Mississippi for two months and I never left the base. Or, I should say I never left to go find any pleasure. I left the base once because I was the duty driver and some guy somehow managed to cut his hand and I had to take him to the hospital. I drove him to the hospital; they patched him up, we came back.

The next time I left the base was to go home on leave. I was happy to leave Mississippi behind. We landed at what must be the world's smallest international airport in Jackson, Mississippi, the Jackson-Medgar Wiley Evers International Airport. It is called an international airport but I don't think it is. One flight to Mexico shouldn't qualify it to be an international airport. That entire airport had no direct flights to anywhere. Every single flight had to go through a hub, either Dallas-Fort Worth or some other nearby hub, like Houston.

My American Airlines flight from DFW landed at LaGuardia in New York City. Goldie came to pick me up; her huge female cousin drove us in her 1994 Navy blue Lexus ES300.

I realized that things were unsettled between us because of all the arguments we'd had while I was in Meridian. While I was in Mississippi Goldie kept telling me, "You need to make an honest woman out of me." I really didn't understand what she was talking about. I had never heard that expression, and the way she said it was very demanding, almost like a "do this or I'll kill you" kind of statement. I finally asked her if that was what she meant and she said, "No, we gotta get married." "What, why?" And then she gave me a bunch of dumb reasons. She kept repeating "You need to make an honest woman out of me." I know now this statement meant, "Please give me all your money and in return I will slowly suck the life out of you. For as long as you're willing to put up with my undiagnosed-mentally-ill ass."

After being confined to base in Great Lakes, after seeing way too many penises and guy-on-guy foreplay in the showers, and then being stationed in Mississippi ... I suffered a momentary lapse in judgment. On December 21, 2012, while on leave before reporting for duty in California, I married Goldie for no reason whatsoever. It was possibly the shortest ceremony I've ever heard of — two witnesses, her father and her grandmother. I didn't have anybody there because, as it was for many other events in my life, I didn't have anybody to invite. That didn't feel weird to me at all; it felt ordinary. It felt familiar. It shouldn't have but it did. Now I realize it was one hundred percent distressing; it shouldn't have been like that, getting married by some random justice of the peace in a poorly-lit city hall annex in the sad city of Bridgeport, CT. After downing at least ten Coors light beers less than two hours prior to the trip from the Howard Johnson in Milford, I got married. I was drunk and could barely stand straight during the ceremony. The rest of the night is a big blur to me. I passed out after drinking more once I got back to the hotel. I experienced the opposite of a HoneyMoon. A moonless "Killer" bees night.

I paid $50 plus $30 for the marriage license and certificate respectively, and $250 to the Puerto Rican lady who married us. I did all of that to allow this freeloader to legally rob me of what would be a million dollars in eight years. I was ultimately giving away my life, all my rights, everything I had, more than half of my money, 80 or 90 percent, to somebody who would never give me anything in return. Not even herself.

After I was conned into marrying Goldie, the end of my days on Earth seemed imminent. Within two days, I contemplated getting an annulment, by January 13, 2013, divorcing her.

The invasion of privacy intensified. Previously, she limited her intrusions to texting or calling new female contacts on my phone. After we moved in together, all social media became fair game. She demanded access to everything and, like a well-trained house boy, I gave her full access. She used that privilege to terrorize EVERYONE. She called, left voicemails, sent text messages, messages on Facebook and Facebook messenger. The worst part of my days became explaining her negative actions to folks. It was as unpleasant as cleaning up a nuclear fallout. I had to deal with this on too many occasions.

I did not see Goldie as someone who could contribute positively in my life; I didn't see her as someone who could have my kid. Not for one second. No way!

Goldie maintains I never did anything for her. That may be true in her mind, but it's far from reality. She is by far the most ungrateful and selfish person I have ever had the misfortune of knowing. I would say she was good for only one thing, sex, but even that was lousy. Our sex life was as exciting as eating mushy and sticky plain white rice boiled without seasoning, not even salt or pepper. Simply put, yawn-worthy, uneventful. It may be due to her unnecessarily inflated ego and her selfish demeanor, or maybe because she's a wannabe rich, spoiled girl trapped in a poor girl's body and life. She felt oddly entitled, and was a very selfish lover. This four-times-a-year bland, lifeless, unexciting sex almost cost me my life.

* * *

My deployment aboard the U.S.S. Nimitz in 2013 was somehow worse than my time in boot camp. I finally saw why we had been tortured the previous year. My command sucked and the people on the boat were less than kind. The entire eighty thousand nautical mile deployment was an experience of a lifetime. Not the good kind. We were used as guinea pigs of the U.S. government. We did a WESTPAC deployment with the sole purpose of going to the South China Sea, Indian Ocean, Arabian Gulf and the Red Sea to protect oil-rich nation states and defend newly formed imperialist friendships. The food was crappy so was the decision to extend us in hell for the world's one percent to keep their wealth and control over every major economy that exists.

One starry night in early October of 2013, around 2:00 a.m., I saw a Russian destroyer following us. It was less than 100 yards away. I knew the ship wasn't American because of its odd proximity, defensive posture, and the fact that most of its lights were still turned on after taps (10:00 p.m.). We were sitting ducks in the Red Sea, doing figure eights and running useless flight ops just to stay busy. We had no business being there because shortly before this, we were relieved by the U.S.S. Ronald Reagan in the Arabian Gulf. For no apparent reason, we stayed in this hot zone. For what? To earn a measly $150 of hazardous duty pay for the month of October? It wasn't worth the potential danger. I heard a rumor going around the boat but I personally hadn't seen it. We were being followed to prevent us from attacking Syria. That's it, we were patsies used by Washington and Moscow. The two nations were playing the political game of "Who can piss further in the snow." We were the pawns being used by the Kings or leaders in their respective capitals. What a joke!

My depression had started long before, sort of like a slow leak of my sanity. Before deployment, I would feel down or anxious for bits of time but I always recovered and carried on. But not until January of 2014, after we came back home, did I really experience severe depression and its debilitating effects on the human body.

Boob-Dado, one of the sailors I served with, advised me to go to Medical, ask for our squadron corpsman and recite these exact words: "I'm not sleeping well, I've been drinking more than usual, I've lost my appetite and I'm no longer enjoying the things that used to bring me joy." After he learned of how I have been feeling.

After I spoke these words to HM1 P., he arranged a consultation for me with the mental health counselors on base at Point Mugu.

The biggest surprise to me when I became a patient was the sheer amount of infrastructure that existed for mental health — psychiatrists, nurse practitioners, nurses, psychologists and an overstocked pharmacy full of pills that were supposed to get me back to mission ready. After all, that's what matters to them, to get me back to work by whatever means necessary.

The process might have worked on anyone else, but it didn't for me. My full-blown depression, anxiety, auditory/visual hallucinations, and mania were not like anybody else's. I was dealing with twenty-five years of repressed emotions. I kept getting worse, the more pills or treatment methods used.

The Navy did not cause me the most harm, much of the damage was done earlier. My childhood was a patchwork of misery and abuse of all kinds. The maltreatments I experienced while on active duty opened the floodgates that allowed all the pent-up feelings to escape from my subconscious to the front of the line. The time spent in uniform accelerated the negative effects of my poor mental health and led to the many related times I was deep in crisis mode. The mental health emergencies I experienced were nothing short of extraterrestrial. All the abuse from my childhood was brought back up, every single wrong I had ever done came to attack my consciousness simultaneously. I had a lot of anger towards those who'd wronged me and toward the people I was serving next to.

Hallucinations, night terrors, nightmares and night sweats attacked me every day from December 2013 to December 2017. None of the medicines they tried worked, including SSRIs (selective serotonin reuptake inhibitors). One of the nurse practitioners I was seeing while I was still on active duty experimented by giving me medicine used as far back as World War I for sailors who'd had similar issues to mine. World War I ended in 1918, over a hundred years ago; he was giving me that medicine because nothing else was working. Nightmares, night terrors, night sweats and an overall lack of interest in living were ever present.

- Marriage -

Goldie and I moved in together ten months after I was assigned to the Golden State. We lived in Camarillo, behind the Elementary School on Las Posas road. We were very close to Malibu, which is right off Pacific Coast Highway. It was easy to take the PCH from LAX (Los Angeles International Airport) to our house. We had a 1650-square-foot, three-bedroom house that we got through the military, which was a lot of house for the two of us. She made sure, before I showed up, the house was fully furnished, using all of the money I had saved while on deployment during most of 2013, leaving me with nothing. I had amassed around twenty thousand dollars in savings while at sea for ten months. But when I came home, I did not have even a thousand dollars left. I had a well-furnished house full of material things, trash and other crap. She is a serious hoarder who is still in denial about her condition. The house was full of trash and the bank accounts were severely depleted. At least mine was; I never had access to hers, and being a hoarder, it wouldn't surprise me if she was siphoning cash from mine to hers. I suspect that is exactly what she did.

She spent money like we were rich, but I was a low-level enlisted person making barely anything. Unlike most military personnel, I didn't get the luxury of keeping the basic allowance for housing. Other married service members would be allotted a thousand dollars for housing; they'd rent a place for around five or six hundred dollars and pocket the difference. Instead, I got us a big old house with a company that was affiliated with the base where we were living. The entire amount of the rent was deducted directly from my check. I never even saw that money. As for the allowance I was given for food, it averaged out to about ten dollars a day per person, approximately three hundred dollars a month.

On my pay of less than $2100 a month, I had to try to please the ungrateful, asexual woman I'd married. I spent my entire pay, everything I had, on her, from the down payment on her car and her monthly car payments to her car insurance for over five years. I asked her to help out, at least with the car insurance, by paying a hundred dollars only, bi-annually. I never got anything. I was ridiculed instead. She laughed at my face.

Oftentimes, wives try to make up for not contributing financially in other ways, such as ... oh, I don't know, being their husband's friend or confident, the person he can turn to when things are tough; or managing the household finances to make sure that in fifty years when they get too old to work, they can stay afloat. I got nothing like that. Sexual favors? I had to pay extra for them — on top of the money I was already paying to support both of us. If I ever wanted sex, or even a back rub or any kind of intimacy, I had to pay extra. It was pay to keep her around, pay to keep her happy, and I had to pay-to-play. To say she was high maintenance and very low reward would be the understatement of this millennia.

Goldie continuously diagnosed herself with all kinds of medical issues. And due to her overuse of over-the-counter medications such as Vagistat and Monistat, she constantly thought she had some type of infection. A yeast infection was her commonly proclaimed self-diagnosis. On more than a handful of occasions, she accused me of passing on a different sexually transmitted disease or infection to her. I had to get tested for those things at least once a year throughout our marriage. I always tested negative because I never engaged in any kind of sexual relationship with anyone else. A few times, I did talk to other women over the phone and online but that was as far as my "infidelity" ever went. No physical contact ever took place. None.

She tested FALSE positive for everything at one point or another, including but not limited to: Chlamydia, Gonorrhea, Herpes, Syphilis, HIV, yeast infections and lastly, Vaginella. The latter was the biggest joke in the world. Vaginella is a women-only infection. It requires a vagina, female reproductive organs and the whole shebang. I never had a vagina or uterus; now you tell me how I gave this woman Vaginella? My doctor told her that it was impossible for me to have given it to her; she was skeptical of his comment and remained convinced that I was unfaithful and it was I, who spread this women-only infection to her using my imaginary, nonexistent vagina. Her vagina was on the fritz all the time. When she somehow contracted Mononucleosis, the kissing disease of careless sexually active teenagers, she was convinced that she would finally be able to pin something on me. To add fuel to her resentment, I once again tested negative for mono.

I felt like I was being forced to rent a terrible film that only played in five-minute increments, with each scene worse than the previous one. Every day, she made everything about her. It was me, me, me, me, me. "Oh, you gave me money yesterday? That was for yesterday's play. You owe me money for today's also." I guess it wasn't illegal because we were married, but it was completely unfair. I should have a way of getting some of that money back. It added up to tens of thousands of dollars every year. One of her typical ways of collecting was: "Oh, I need to add some fake extensions to my hair; these are real human hair from some country in East Asia," I have a feeling, young adults were being shaved against their wills so they can make fake hair for this woman to put on her head for one or two months, then toss the hair in the trash. They were expensive, up to a thousand dollars and she'd buy them every month or so. Then, she'd pay three or four hundred dollars more to have them attached. She was paying around $1300 every six weeks for fake hair. I'd be lucky if she kept them for two months. She also had wigs. Her hair was constantly being done.

The reward I got from being her sole supporter, the person making sure that she looks so good that people are giving her excessive compliments, was that sometimes she'd show me her middle finger and remind me that I'm a lucky guy because she had to lower her standards to marry me. What standards? She claimed superiority because she went to a mediocre 4-year college. She went to college to get a third-tier higher education experience from a second-tier school, and come out with first-tier student loans. How pathetic!

The expression, "I picked her up from the gutter" is our real story. When I met her, she lived in the worst project in Bridgeport. The Beardsley Terrace was frightful and dangerous, the cops were scared to go there. Food deliveries ceased to take place there because it was too perilous for the drivers. Murders occurred on a weekly basis, with random intermittent violent crimes sprinkled here and there. One night, I was walking Goldie home after a gala in Milford when we got mugged at gunpoint. It was a cool, starry night with a full moon. He was not visible when we left my 1996 off-white Lexus ES 300. We were a few steps from her gate when he jumped out and yelled at us to stop walking. He kept saying, "run the cash, run it all." That's robbery talk for "give me all your money." He wore a black ski mask over his mouth, nose, and neck. This mask was more often used during the winter months for more benign purposes. He chose to wear it to rob us that breezy night. His head was covered by some kind of hat. The gun was chrome and shinier than any other gun I have ever seen. It could have been due to its extremely close proximity to my forehead. The barrel was cold and the young gunman appeared scared and conflicted. He was shaking. I don't exactly know why but I wasn't as scared as he looked. All I had was $16 in single dollar bills. I pleaded with the masked gunman; I wanted to give him five or so dollars. He cocked the gun back when I started arguing with him. I was in between jobs at the time; those dollar bills felt like individual stocks in Amazon or Berkshire Hathaway. His eyes didn't have the look of a serial robber or thief; he looked like a high school kid. A desperate kid wanting to make some quick bucks in a system stacked against the youth, especially the poor ones living in the hood. I didn't blame him. I knew the place was dangerous. I accepted this fate when I ingeniously decided to date some ultra basic bottom feeder from there. That was my fault. I deserved this. Maybe this was the only way he knew to feed himself or his younger siblings. Maybe he had to support a drug addiction or something along those lines. I don't judge, nor will I sound like I knew him, or him me. He knew her though. He knew her well because he kept calling her over to him and saying: "Hey shawty, shawty, let me holla at you." Over and over, I heard the first few times. She tentatively walked away as they continued this exchange for over two minutes, according to Goldie. All she kept saying to him was; "No, I live right here, I'm gonna go inside my house now." After taking my wallet and keys he ordered me to run. I ran the other direction and disappeared in the tall buildings adorned with brick. The young gunman was only interested in getting her phone number after he successfully chased me away in front of her tiny front gate and yard. Maybe she gave him her number, I'm very hesitant of how she got free and, unblemished, walked inside her safe home ten feet away from where this happened. It wouldn't surprise me if she did. I will never know.

I took her from that environment to Camarillo, California, a contrasting living situation. Was she grateful to me? No, never. Not only was she ungrateful, she did absolutely nothing to improve the quality of my life. I didn't want to be treated like a god or a king. I merely wanted, just once, to be acknowledged as the sole reason that she was enjoying a wonderful life in Southern California in a county where the average yearly temperature is between sixty-five to seventy degrees. It would get hot for only about one week a year. And the cold? The coldest it gets is forty-five degrees Fahrenheit. What appreciation did I ever get for putting Goldie in this situation? Absolutely none.

Unfortunately, I turned to the bottle and started drinking heavily and excessively. From January 1st, 2014 to December 31st, 2017, I had at least one drink every day. I quickly built up a tolerance. Towards the later part of that time frame, my drinking escalated more and more. At times I would pass out on the stairs. Goldie would step over me and go upstairs to sleep. If I passed out on the couch, sometimes she'd take the almost empty bottle out of my hand; sometimes she wouldn't, depending on her mood. I was consuming up to 20 beers or three bottles of red wine per day. I had to drink them all in less than three hours or the buzz would run away from me and I wouldn't be able to fall asleep all night. I wasn't eating, I wasn't sleeping, I wasn't living. I was a complete mess physically and especially mentally. I was slowly dying. She loved seeing me like that. She could care less that my life was about to be over.

Goldie did whatever she could to make sure that I felt life wasn't worth living. As far as doing anything to help me become a better person, a better man, by being there for me, trying to understand what I'd gone through, understanding what happened to me after I came back from deployment and I didn't want to live anymore, she had no interest in that. On a few occasions she deliberately made things worse by calling my command to complain about me, making a false report, making it sound like I was doing something to her. She lied to them.

She claimed she wanted to get me help. I asked her, "Why don't you help me yourself?" She said, "I'm not gonna do that. That's not what I'm here for. Go talk to your doctor. I'm your wife; I'm not your friend."

To her, our marriage was a business decision; we were colleagues and this was a business deal. A Joint Venture. A bad one at that. She constantly claimed my emotional intelligence was subpar. I asked her; "Please help me, please show what someone with superior emotional intelligence is supposed to be like or act like."

By the time I got the full sentence out she was usually out the door or already upstairs watching one of those ridiculous reality shows she loved so dearly. The premise of the shows and the content was often dumb, so were the all cast members.

She never wanted to help me in that aspect, she only wanted to remind me at least once a week that: My emotional intelligence was shit and she's not putting up with me until it improves. She never showed me this superior intellect of hers. I was there to be blamed for EVERYTHING. That's all. Also, she's superior to me in every way imaginable. I was the piece of crap that needed constant fixing and her, the Perfect Queen. A perfect individual, flawless even. She kept the insults short at times; she would say: "Fix your EQ" and vanish into the day or night, floating away as the wind affably carried her Royal Highness off of the floor. I was nothing, a commoner or peasant in the presence of royalty.

She was never my friend; she was just someone using me for whatever opportunities and potential I might have. If she could get something out of the relationship, she was all for it, but the minute things started going sideways, even before that happened, she removed herself from me completely.

She would go hang out on the beach in Santa Barbara all day when I was hurting and needing someone to talk to. No. She was never there. Unless I didn't want to talk, then she would make sure that I had to speak with her. Anything I ever wanted, Goldie wanted the opposite. When I needed some time by myself, that's when she would insist, "I need to talk to you; if you don't want to talk to me I'm going to call your command and get you in more trouble." When I wanted to talk, she referred me to a friend. She would say: "I'm your wife, not your friend. Don't talk to me about these things, call a friend or something and get out of my face."

I'm not telling you this to complain; I'm openly sharing what I went through with this woman who was imbibing the life out of me like a parasitic leech. I understand, leeches often feed on coagulated blood that's non-circulating, but she voraciously gulped the fresh blood that my heart had just pumped out that was providing oxygen to my brain. She made sure that my brain was deprived of oxygen and the nutrients it needed by sticking her fangs in me and guzzling my life force and my will to live. I was walking around, but I was lifeless. I wasn't living, I merely existed. I was a dead man walking.

I was numb, soulless, lifeless. I gave up on personal hygiene altogether. For months, due to the stench, she had to remind me to shower. I was dead inside and out. She loved this tamed and subjugated version of me that didn't cause her any worry of potential infidelity. During that time, I had to beg to get her to spend any time with me.

By the end of summer 2014, I was spiraling out of control. I went to work hungover every day. I somehow managed to get the job done while operating on less than ten percent mental capacity. At times, I had many daytime out-of-body experiences while at work, and things were getting worse and worse. As a plane captain, the job I did was very dangerous but I never caused harm to myself or anyone else. I thank the universe and my grandma for safeguarding me and those around me.

From October 1st to December 30, 2014, I had four hospitalizations in an inpatient psychiatric hospital. Each stay involved two different places, beginning at Vista del Mar in the hills of Ventura, and later transferring via ambulance to the Naval Medical Center in San Diego for further evaluation. The shortest combined stay was seven days and the longest lasted three weeks.

The first time I was hospitalized was due to my first-ever suicide attempt. My command was about to go on another useless exercise in the Pacific Ocean, a RIMPAC-like exercise aboard the Nimitz. Earlier that day, the nurse practitioner had prescribed me the last of the WW1-era SSRIs, which I hadn't yet taken.

A feeling of uselessness and emptiness suddenly overwhelmed me. I saw the walls closing in on me, literally. I know now it was a hallucination, but it felt very real. It was a crisp clear night, I went out to the yard for some fresh air. I could hear neighbors to the left and right of our house laughing and having a ball in their respective yards. As the night air filled my lungs, the pungent smell of rotten cabbage from the cabbage farm down the road was unpleasant.

I swallowed two of the 30 pills I'd been given. I felt nothing. I waited a few minutes and took another. I was crying while taking the pills one by one every three minutes. I took eleven, ten more than the prescribed daily dosage. I felt all alone, out of place. Then a feeling of calmness spread throughout my being. The world was about to be made better by my impending exit from it. Thoughts flitted briefly through my mind: What will my neighbors think when they find out how I died? Will they wonder if they could have helped me if they'd known? Will my mother cry? I wasn't seeing clearly anymore, my vision was fading more with each labored breath. I slipped away into the darkness. It was weirdly relaxing. I felt unbound.

Suddenly, an odd burst of energy jolted me awake to find myself lying on the living room floor, sweating profusely and gasping for air. I felt like I'd died and been resuscitated. Consciousness returned gradually. I realized I was wearing only boxer shorts and a t-shirt. I remembered the pills. I dialed 911 and told the operator, "I took some pills and now I don't wanna die anymore." She repeated my address, and asked me to open the front door. I opened it and blacked out again. When I woke up, paramedics were working on me. I saw a sheriff's deputy going upstairs with his boots on. I tried to protest: Really guy? You're not gonna take off your shoes in my house? Wow! Instead, my eyes closed again and the sounds were gone. I traversed to another dimension.

I woke up the next morning, choking. I couldn't breathe. There was a tube down my throat. I couldn't raise my arms. My hands were tied to the bed, by my side. A kind nurse noticed I was awake and told me the paramedics had to intubate me because I hadn't been breathing well enough. My breaths were very faint, she said. My hands were tied because I had kept trying to remove the tubes in my sleep. I was in Saint John's Hospital Intensive Care Unit in Camarillo.

The evil woman was next to me, pretending to be a loving wife. She acted as if things were perfect and I wasn't sick to the point of trying to take my own life. She acted so kindly towards me in the hospital, I started to believe the lies she was vocalizing to the hospital staff and the Ventura County Crisis Team that came to interview me to assess whether or not I needed further evaluation.

Of course, she is a fraud who was lying to make herself appear healthy and sane, and me deranged. True, I had wanted to take my own life partly because of experiences unrelated to her, but the main reason was her. She made my life so wretched that it wasn't worth living. Death had seemed preferable to sharing a roof with her for one more night. She was intolerable. Too much to handle.

I had survived, but I continued to be in terrible shape emotionally. I suffered unbearable remorse for the tiniest infraction I'd ever been part of. I carried the burden of guilt for Psychopath's many rampages on our family. I felt the weight of the world on my shoulders. I was ashamed of myself; my confidence and self-esteem were at an all-time low.

My home life became more and more insufferable. The fights happened more often than ever before. Goldie completely checked out and gave up on me. She knew what was gonna happen. She knew where I was headed.

To an early grave. I was gonna die of cirrhosis or liver failure and then she was gonna take her half million dollars of life insurance and find a new guy. She told me straight out that was her plan: "What else would you want me to do? I will pay off the house and remarry right away." I couldn't believe her cruelty. She could have at least lied to me until I died.

The hallucinations intensified. On December 9, 2014, I attempted to take my own life once more. I had a secret stash of antidepressants that I'd heard could get the job done. During my first stay in San Diego, another patient told me that 50 of the 100 mg pills would do the job in less than five hours.

I counted the pills, I had 65 in total. I had some liquor left in the fridge, a gallon jug of Carlo Rossi White Zinfandel that was a quarter full. I took a big gulp of the wine and started to stuff my face with a generous handful of pills. I couldn't swallow them; my throat was too dry, and I was nauseated because I'd drunk the other three quarters of the gallon bottle the night before. I couldn't get the pills down so I went to the trash can and threw them up; they were wet and breaking apart from being in my mouth for so long. There were at least 21 pills in the trash can.

I continued drinking the rest of the wine and, midway through, I remembered that I needed to make amends with someone I had hurt very much. Her name was Carpe Diem; we'd dated for a brief period from 2007 to 2008. I had cheated on Goldie with her. I didn't want to do it, but the devil took over my soul during those times; I was acting more and more like Psychopath. Carpe Diem was there for me long before anyone else in this country ever showed me what it meant to have somebody's back. I knew she was hurt by my actions, and I thought to call her one last time to ask for her forgiveness. I also told her the whole truth about me and Goldie. Everything I had hidden for years. She was very angry at me but she could sense that, given my current state of mind, it wasn't the time to yell at me. The kind of intuition Goldie lacks. I informed Carpe Diem that I was sorry for all the hurt I had caused her and told her that she no longer had to worry about me doing that to another soul because "today is the day I will take my own life and leave you behind.

The world will be better without me in it."

She asked if I was drunk; I said yes. I reassured her that although the pills couldn't go down, I was going to use a knife to pierce through my heart, therefore making the world a much better place. One with me removed. She pleaded with me not to do it, but I wasn't looking for someone to talk me off the ledge. My mind was made up. I simply wanted to apologize to her for the hurt I'd caused.

I hung up the phone, finished the big jug of Carlo Rossi white zin, and grabbed the long and slim filet knife to go complete my narrative. I wanted it to be a big surprise to my unsuspecting dreadful wife, I thought, What better way to go than in the back of my new, white 2013 Dodge Dart SXT? I grabbed a decorative pillow from the sofa; I opened the garage door; I opened the trunk of the car and climbed in. As I started to bring the knife towards my heart, a feeling of freedom, carelessness and relaxation came over me. Abruptly, I felt my grandma's presence. She didn't want me to do it. I couldn't go through with it. At the time, my Dart's name was Rose. I thought about my grandma the entire time I was in the trunk until I passed out and was awoken by a mob of people: two Ventura County sheriff deputies who were unbothered, Goldie, four paramedics, and a loud siren from the ambulance that wasn't helping my headache. This escapade led to my longest, and last, psych ward stay.

After being admitted for my third stay in San Diego, the hospital's officer-in-charge or OIC, who was an O-6, or Captain in the Navy, came across my file. He realized that my many stays at his hospital were consistent with someone who was unable to handle the extremely stressful job of active duty personnel. Clearly I couldn't get the help I needed while on active duty. He sent a letter to my commanding officer and recommended that I be relieved of military service and processed out immediately. This happened at the end of November 2014. The process started, as did my uncertainty for the future.

* * *

One morning in early spring 2015, around 11 a.m., Goldie ran over my right forearm with her back driver's side tire. I was feeling lonely and isolated and I asked her to stay with me. Freshly discharged from the Navy, I wasn't working, and I was tired of drinking Coors light or Carlo Rossi White Zinfandel while watching Dexter, Sons of Anarchy or Weeds on Netflix. She was trying to leave for Santa Barbara to get away from me. She ran over my arm and kept on driving; she returned after the sun went down. The neighbors saw me writhing on the ground in pain; I was too embarrassed to tell them what had happened. I simply laid there until the pain traveled down to my fingers.

I knew she had seen me behind her car. I laid directly behind her car at first; she threatened to run over my entire body if I didn't move away. She later told me she needed to get to Santa Barbara to be around good and normal people. She never apologized for running me over; she exclaimed; "Even if I ran over your whole body, it would have been your fault; therefore, I have nothing to be sorry for."

She was never sorry for anything. She still maintains complete and utter innocence of everything that went wrong between us. As per our last conversation, she has never done anything wrong, and everything that went wrong was my fault. She's "as innocent as a brand-new baby" — her words.

* * *

While I'm not necessarily proud of my many stints in the loony bin, at the same time I'm glad they happened because they allowed me to get the help I needed and, more importantly, took me away from Goldie. During those times, she could not hurt me. She couldn't contact me because there were no phone calls in and out, unless I personally wanted to make a phone call to her, a very rare occurrence.

I'm sure that in a way she felt relieved; these separations were vacations for her. Each hospitalization lasted at least a week, I was away for about a month and a half total during that three-month span. Of course, while I was gone, she continued spending money as if the two of us were still going out.

I got out of the service, but the panic attacks, anxiety attacks, depression, high anxiety, hallucinations both auditory and visual, continued wherever I went. They were happening more often than not; on a daily basis I'd get around ten hallucinations, both auditory and visual. The nightmares never went away. Three central characters were ever present in them: the incompetent flight surgeon that was my supposed doctor; the entire group of people I had worked with at the VAW E-2 squadron and the woman I shared a bed with.

Dr. S.F., the flight surgeon, was the dumbest individual I had known at the time. He was as clueless as a doorknob. At one point, I wanted to hurt him. I have since asked the universe to forgive me for those negative thoughts I had about him. I haven't had these thoughts in years and I hope he forgives me for having them.

The VAW squadron I was assigned to was by far the worst work environment I have ever been a part of. It felt like most of the people there were criminals given a choice by a judge to go to prison or join the military. That's how incompetent there were. Inappropriate relationships triumphed there while real talent was ignored by those in charge. The commanding and executive officers were unaware of the toxicity that existed during my time there. First Classes, Chiefs and Senior Chiefs were cheating on their wives with lower-ranking enlisted personnel. Sailors did all types of drugs regularly, including cocaine. It was there where I learned cocaine is fast acting and leaves the body without a trace in less than fifty hours. A handful of blue jackets discussed it openly at my house when we got back from deployment. They snorted cocaine while in San Francisco that spring. The young officers were spoiled and entitled, yet couldn't even change the oil in the very aircraft they were flying every day.

When I thought things couldn't get worse, especially since the biggest waste of skin, a senior chief, Christopher, had left the squadron in the spring of 2014, they did. We got a new executive officer; he was formerly enlisted and talked like his shit didn't stink. XO2 was as terrible as they came. He somehow kissed and licked enough butts to get to where he was and openly expected everyone to return the favor to him. Lastly, we had a six-foot-eight Command Master Chief who was a walking military sexual trauma poster. He would whisper in my ear and hug me until I felt his boner. His hugs were long and uncomfortable; they could last as long as a minute, while he spoke very softly into my ear. At times, he also held my hands during this pathetically sad ordeal. He blew warm air into the ears of all lower ranked enlisted personnel. He was the senior enlisted person for our command. We had nowhere to go complain about him and his creepy ways. What a creep! A picture-taking tall scumbag.

Those were the main players in my ever-recurring nightmares. In my dreams, they would chase me down, trying to kill me. I was always running away from them to prevent my death. My wonderful wife appeared as an alternate whenever the other characters would take a break. Her appearances grew over time as the others faded away.

I was still having the dreams until October 2019, when I psychologically kicked her out of my head for good. I took all of the power back from her and she no longer controls my real life or subconscious. The last straw was when she claimed that I gave her H. Pylori; that claim I rejected wholeheartedly, telling her to take her accusations back where they came from because I would no longer accept her unfounded finger pointing.

That was the last infection she accused me of passing on to her before I filed for divorce and stopped getting involved with her sexually. I know my status; it is all green lights all around. I have nothing, I gave nothing.

- Leaving -

A few months after leaving the Navy, I began working at a premier golf-centered country club in Camarillo, California. It boasted an enormous clubhouse, over 44,000 square feet, and the property included a lot of acreage.

The job itself wasn't hard, but it was really hard for me to do any job because of my chaotic home life. I didn't have any peace or any safe place where I could escape the constant turmoil. Life could never be normal because of the person I was sharing my home with.

Despite what I was going through, I managed to buckle down and work really, really hard, and within a few months I was promoted to the mid-level management team. This was a long-sought goal for me as I'd worked in the hospitality industry for a while, and before joining the service, I'd earned my degree in hospitality management.

One of the drawbacks of the work environment was a serious lack of professionalism. In fact, professionalism did not exist there. I don't know if it was through ignorance or indifference, but I was wrongly criticized by my boss, DonJulio, for being too professional. More than once, he pulled me aside and chided me for not socializing enough with the staff. He told me, "I want you to open up, let them all into your personal life like I have." He bragged that his personal life was an open book to the entire staff. I completely disagreed with this management style and I did not comply with his requests. It was true that I didn't put my personal life on public display, and I didn't invite staff to my house for drinks like he did. He kept reminding me, "People say they don't know who you are."

I thought, This is ridiculous because they do know who I am. I am right here looking at them, talking to them on a daily basis. And the worst part? They were snakes. Hypocritically, they would eat with me, laugh with me, hang out the entire day, and as soon as I'd leave, they'd go right to DonJulio's office to complain about me. They'd say that I was doing the work that they should be doing, that I didn't trust them to do their jobs. DonJulio would confront me about what they'd said, I'd try to explain myself to the employees: "It's not that I don't trust you. I like a working position; I like to get my hands dirty; I like to be involved, that's just the way I am." But they didn't understand that, I think partly because DonJulio was never hands-on. He would show up and say, "Oh, you guys got it?" And he'd be gone like the wind. I really don't have much respect for bosses who do that. But they were so used to his style of management that my style seemed weird, and apparently the fact that I didn't have a habit of caressing women's faces made me seem unfriendly. Like they said: Too professional.

DonJulio was very touchy-feely. I would see him stroking the women's faces, hands, arms. What I considered sexual harassment and inappropriate touching, he considered getting to know the staff. It was completely sophomoric behavior and it wasn't directed only at females. He'd grab younger male employees and jab his fingers in their butts, or give them uncomfortable hugs and I even saw him grab their genitals. DonJulio would then tell me to loosen up because I was too stiff.

I wanted to tell him, "DonJulio, you could probably learn something from me because you're going to catch a lawsuit for those horrendous things you're doing. You'll get into some serious trouble if you continue touching employees the way you are and making sexually charged comments." I didn't say anything to him because he was always thumping me and I had no say.

If DonJulio had ever attended a single college-level course in hospitality management, he would have learned that some things that were permissible in the seventies, eighties and nineties cannot be done anymore because times have changed. Besides, we shouldn't objectify any women regardless of how much men like DonJulio believe they like and welcome that kind of attention. No one should be treated like that. Even if they think it's okay, we need to change the norm, stop treating them that way, re-educate them. Instead of criticizing me because I wasn't sexually harassing women, DonJulio should have taken a page out of my book and started treating everyone with respect regardless of color, race, gender, or sexual orientation.

Dealing with DonJulio became more difficult, and the rift between us continued to grow. By the end of November 2015, I guess he'd had it, and he asked me to sit down for a meeting. DonJulio summoned me to one of the upper manager's offices, where he sat behind the desk as if we weren't cool anymore and he needed to be really formal. I sat across from him, the same guy who'd been telling me I needed to sexually assault female staff members because they didn't know me well enough. DonJulio handed a couple of papers across the desk. One of them listed various liquor prices, and another document that he said was very important, a six-page training manual for new managers. This manual outlined procedures that were to be followed for the first ninety days of employment. It covered everything I was supposed to do daily. There were checklists of the various duties that my trainer was supposed to follow with me. Both the trainer and I should have signed these papers during my training period.

DonJulio was supposed to have been my trainer for my first 90 days of employment. I started working as the Food and Beverage Manager on August 16. At the end of November, over 100 days later, this ineffective manager handed me the training material. He told me I needed to start following the manual from that point on.

I wanted to know if he was going to be the trainer specified in the manual. He said, "On your own; you need to follow this manual from this point forward and let me know when you're done with all the tasks."

I went home and read the material. I was baffled. The training manual was well planned out and it explicitly stated that a trainer was required to accompany the new manager throughout the initial 90 days. That had never happened. I had to be the trainer and the trainee because DonJulio was inept.

I got to a point the following year, shortly before the summer, that I realized I'd had enough of DonJulio and his abused minions. I'd had enough at home also. I kept having daytime nightmares — not daydreams but day nightmares, "daymares." I felt I could not take it anymore. The medicine they were giving me wasn't helping; alcohol wasn't working anymore. I was hallucinating more than twenty times per day. I was hallucinating at work. Even if I was there for only a couple of hours I'd have several hallucinations. One of my recurring hallucinations was that I was having a panic attack. Wherever I was standing, my mind imagined me lying on the floor in the fetal position, unable to catch my breath, not knowing what's happening to me. It wasn't a physical thing; it was a psychological issue that was manifesting itself in a physical manner. I didn't suffer any attacks there, I constantly had elevated anxiety levels over having the attacks. Weird, I know.

I quit the job, with no other jobs lined up. When I gave notice, DonJulio appeared extremely disappointed. I didn't understand his reaction because he was constantly calling me out on things that I wasn't even doing wrong. He had been particularly angry to learn that I was doing the work of five workers on Mondays during the golf tournaments. I believe the big boss, El Jefe had taunted him about how well I worked with him compared to DonJulio. They had an odd sibling-like rivalry. They cared for one another but jumped at the chance to embarrass each other in front of others. It seemed weird to me, but the relationship worked for them, I guess. On Mondays, regardless of the size of the golf tournament, there would be only three of us in the morning. At times, we needed six or more workers but we had to make do with three. One time, only two us finished a tournament due to a staff member being sent home early. That tournament was enormous, we needed at least seven workers there, the vendors were very difficult to deal with. It was only Sheldon and me. Sheldon was a skinny white kid with a very positive can-do attitude. A hard worker, in my book, who came through in the clutch for the club many times. After that guy yelled at him and the other worker, it really hurt me because I was there every Monday and I knew how hard we worked to make sure ALL the tournaments were successful regardless of our staffing shortcomings.

Did I work harder on Mondays? Yes! Was there ever adequate staff on Mondays? NO! We were ALWAYS understaffed on Mondays. It helped that El Jefe knew I was up for the job; he trained me one week and the next week he checked on me and asked if I was ok; I told him yes and I said, "You should go home, sir; from now on, I got it on Mondays." The hours were also much longer on Mondays. I typically went in around seven or eight in the morning, and the earliest I ever left was 6:00 p.m. One Monday in March of 2016, I worked from 6:30 to 10:15 p.m. There were some complications with scheduling and the evening staff was short. I made myself the extra guy to augment our manpower. After seeing how hard we worked to pull off another terrific tournament, I called my car wash guy and personally paid to have six cars washed that night. The cars belonged to the staff that had showed up. They were speechless. I told them not to say anything to anyone. Certainly NOT to DonJulio or El Jefe, but wouldn't you know it? They must have told them because that Wednesday, DonJulio told me to watch what I say and watch what I do for the staff. I paid to get their cars washed; I asked them to keep it between us; they didn't, they caused DonJulio to yell at me once more. Would I do it again? Yes. I would pay for their car wash again today if I had to. It was a tough day for all of us. When I got home, I was so tired, I didn't need the usual ten to fifteen beers to put me out. My sleep problems were forced to relax, as were my hallucinations and daymares. They disappeared because I didn't have any time to focus on myself. No time for my brain to play tricks on me.

Once I quit, I spent some time calibrating the stuff I needed to. I was drinking more because the sleep I needed for my body to recover never came without alcohol. When I did fall asleep, I would wake up in the air-conditioned room sweating like I'd been playing soccer for hours under the hot sun.

It seemed I couldn't get out from under these tight constraints. I had left the job; now I started to think of an exit strategy from my wife. In the meantime, we bought a house. Things got worse. The minute I put Goldie in a house, she started doing even less than she had before. Her favorite statements now were, "I'm a housewife; I have a house. I'm a wife. I don't have to do that anymore." That meant anything and everything. You name it. She wasn't doing it.

I'm not kinky. I don't ask for weird sexual favors. I'm a normal guy with normal desires and expectations. But because her ultimate goals were to take as much from me as she possibly could, she refused everything — unless I paid her. It got to the point where a sexual encounter with her would cost me upwards of $2700. At that price, I was only able to buy sex three or four times a year — from my wife. We were married, therefore, no matter how much financial abuse I suffered, it was not a crime. In my book, she was a criminal operating under the protection of the law, sort of like an undercover cop who gets involved in illegal activities, but because it is in their job description, it's okay.

In 2017, shortly before my birthday, I bought a Samsung Galaxy S8+ cellular phone. A new phone meant Goldie could no longer snoop and spy on me. To counter this hurdle, she gifted me a Samsung Gear 3 watch that was compatible with my phone. The watch was a spying tool disguised as a birthday gift. For months, she used the watch to bypass the password on my phone and regain total unhindered access to it. I'm unable to say how many times she spied on me during the next several months. I can report that she was always aware of everything, and I was completely dumbfounded by her precise dictation of my text conversations. I don't know how or when she had the time to do this, but her unscrupulous plan worked. She took the watch back before the Spring of 2018.

That was my Goldie. She treated me like crap, took everything I had. I had nothing left, not even my dignity because she took that with her too. She took my penis because I wasn't able to use it with her and I couldn't use it with anybody else, therefore she had full control of that as well. She had my money, my peace of mind, my penis, and my dignity. All I had left was an empty soul, an empty vessel with absolutely nothing in it. My thoughts, I felt, weren't even mine because they were way too wild for me. I'd never experienced thoughts like that in my entire life. It wasn't a good situation to be in.

* * *

On November 17th of 2017, the doctor informed me that my liver was badly inflamed and I was headed towards cirrhosis. What made things worse for my liver was that I was mixing my meds with the alcohol; this only intensified the damage and was leading to my impending death. Goldie's dreams and wishes were about to come true. My overall health was in shambles. I was overweight, and liver failure, heart attack or stroke were all on the table. I didn't want any of them to be my kryptonite.

I decided to take control and change the course of my life. I wanted to get sober to give my body a fighting chance against the mountain of medical issues I was suffering from.

I told the doctor I would stop drinking, and a month later, I did. On December 31st, 2017, I consumed my last alcoholic drink.

I did it for myself. Goldie didn't care, she'd said so to me many times. With the help of Mr. S.S., my readjustment counselor at the Ventura Vet Center and my VA-appointed psychiatrist at the Oxnard Community-Based Outpatient Clinic, I had all the support I needed to kick that terrible habit. I haven't had to go to a single meeting of any kind for help. I relied on those two individuals and lots of free will to keep the liquor at bay.

The first three months were hell; the withdrawal symptoms almost killed me. I experienced hot flashes like a menopausal woman, abdominal pain, cramps, random stinky sweats, and uneasy feelings that took me to the deepest depths of misery. I nearly lost my mind and the will to live once again. Still, I persevered. I never gave up because I knew that on the other side things would be much sweeter, and if I kept going, I would live to tell my story and hopefully help others get and stay sober.

Now that I've got my sea legs under me, I want to keep going for as long as possible. I have been sober for more than two years now. My sobriety is something I am extremely proud of and I plan on keeping it that way. My liver functions are back to normal. My high blood pressure, high triglycerides and other physical problems have also disappeared. I have first hand knowledge of the dangers associated with alcohol and the fact that it is the real gateway drug, not marijuana. Contrary to what many phony experts claim.

Not long ago I finally took the first step to legally remove myself from Goldie permanently. While waiting for the house to be sold, I left for my own safety and to maintain my hard-fought sobriety.

It is a bit rough at the moment. She's making it harder every day, but I'm gonna keep fighting in the courts. Because I have to get out. I cannot stay. I cannot remain her slave. I cannot remain attached to someone who wants nothing to do with me physically or emotionally but wants all my money, even future money, even money twenty years from now. Why does she think she deserves whatever money I earn? I don't know. I will never understand it. That was her mindset. Her way.

One month before I filed for divorce, my male cousin Chalien called me at 4:31 a.m. from Bohio, where he lives. I've tried to explain the three-hour time difference to him many times, but he can never seem to grasp it. I slept through the call and Goldie woke me up violently, yelling, kicking and shaking me. She looked like the Devil awakened in the middle of his beauty sleep. She furiously demanded: "Who the FUCK is Charlene?! Are you fucking her?!" I was out of it, given the time; I looked at the phone and saw it was my male cousin calling. I told her, "Your crazy is showing; get a hold of yourself, this is my male cousin," and went back to bed. Although she was wrong and her behavior was clearly out of line, for days she walked around the house acting like I was the culprit and this guiltless call was blown out of proportion by me.

In my eyes, Goldie was nothing but a starter wife. Someone/something I was supposed to experience before I am allowed to meet my true Queen and partner to do life with. The experiment is over! Where are you, girl?

I dream about her sometimes. She is everything Goldie isn't, kind, understanding, caring and sweet. In my dreams, our home is bigger than the one I had to sell after I filed for divorce in 2019. We will have it all, I know it. I can't wait for those glorious days because heaven knows, I've experienced some very rough patches. I need a good woman in my life, I'm overdue for one. I'm not getting any younger. I will treat her right. I will be a great husband to her, I know the feeling will be totally reciprocated. She will be my light and I, hers. My better half. The relationship will be similar to that of Melinda and Bill Gates. The Obamas. I will be her Dwayne Wade and she will be my Gabrielle Union-Wade. I love me some Gabrielle! I love me some Ms. Independent.

All of this will be possible because the Universe has spoken. On Tuesday February 18th, 2020 at 9:49 a.m., my divorce was finalized. At 10:01 a.m., in room 30, at the Ventura County Superior Courthouse, we received our copies of the filed documents, relieving me of all future agony and misery. I overpaid for the two envelopes to mail us our official Notice of Dissolution of Marriage. I paid $7 for two envelopes, including hers. I paid for her needs one last time. I have been a FREE man for 69 days now. As for the IRS, they classify me as single with no dependents. Tax experts say; that is the worst tax bracket to be in, I love being there for now. I don't think there is a word to describe how I feel. All of the world's dictionaries are lacking such words. I won the biggest prize that exists. I feel as if I just won the Mr. Universe contest. Since such a contest doesn't exist, I claimed the title unchallenged and unopposed. Please call me Mr. Universe 2020. Because I WON my freedom fair and square. Please refer to me as the BIG WINNER from now on. #Mruniverse2020 #winning.

- About the Author -

Verly (SonSonn) spent the first 17 years of his life in Haiti. He is a nature and an animal lover. He enjoys meeting interesting people. The most influential person in his life is and forever will be his maternal grandma, Rose. Shortly after immigrating to the United States at age 17, he was left to fend for himself. His quality of life in Bridgeport, Connecticut was subpar, at best. Yet he continued to financially and emotionally support his family back home to the best of his ability. Verly is a fighter, and despite life's many obstacles, he managed to put himself through school. He currently holds degrees in Hospitality Management and Business Administration. He has worked a variety of odd jobs, often more than one simultaneously to try and get ahead in life. To show his gratitude to his new homeland, in his mid-twenties he volunteered to join the United States Navy. He considered this decision to be an absolutely necessary means of proudly displaying his patriotic spirit. Verly currently resides in Los Angeles, California.

www.ingramcontent.com/pod-product-compliance
Lightning Source LLC
Chambersburg PA
CBHW070431010526
44118CB00014B/1996